The Collected
Poems of
Dilys Laing

The
Collected
Poems of
Dilys
Laing

With an Introduction
by M. L. Rosenthal

THE PRESS OF CASE WESTERN RESERVE UNIVERSITY

1967

Printed in the United States of America by the Oberlin Printing
Company, Oberlin, Ohio.

Library of Congress Catalogue Card Number 67-14519.

ACKNOWLEDGMENTS

Most of the poems in this collection were first printed in the periodicals listed below. Grateful acknowledgment is made for assignments of copyright and for permissions to reprint. Translations from *Paroles* by Jacques Prévert have been included with the kind consent of M. Prévert and of his publishers, Librairie Gallimard, Le Point du Jour, N.R.F. Poems which first appeared in *Walk Through Two Landscapes* (1949) are here reprinted with the kind assent of Twayne Publishers, Inc. Thanks also are due the Macmillan Company for permission to reprint two sections of *Poems from a Cage* (1961).

ANGRY PENGUINS. "Maidanek, Dachau, Buchenwald"; "Who Is Not Who."

ANGRY PENGUINS BROADSHEET. "Ocean Fable."

APPROACH. "Poem" ("The still air . . ."); "Declaration of War on Me."

THE ATLANTIC MONTHLY. "Lost, Stolen, Strayed"; "The Poet and His Poem"; "Trial by Fury"; "Walk Through Two Landscapes."

THE BELOIT POETRY JOURNAL. "Profane Witness."

THE CARLETON MISCELLANY. "And Bill Made the Beast of the Earth"; "Come with Me to Korea, Miss Smith"; "Comforter"; "Dark Death"; "False Move, or Fair"; "Fertility Rite"; "Final Verdict"; "Fish"; "For It Is Better to Marry than to Burn"; "For What We Are About to Receive"; "Forgive Me"; "Fragment" ("Sleep, soft murderer . . ."); "Fragment" ("You warn of hell . . ."); "Holbein Goblin"; "How Music's Made"; "I-Thou"; "The Idols"; "Ikons of Myself"; "In a Dry Season"; "Last Discipline"; "Mexican Hill Farmers"; "Miao"; "New Saw"; "Note"; "Song of One Burden Bearer to Another"; "Stabat Mater"; "Storm Near Lesbos"; "The Traveller"; "Worker."

CHATELAINE. "Dig No Hole"; "Violin"; "Walking."

THE CHURCHMAN. "Bird of Easter."

COMMONWEAL. "Carol to Be Sung to Lutes or Banjos."

CONTEMPORARY POETRY. "Not According to Plan."

THE DARTMOUTH. "Ignis Dominae"; "Scape-Grace"; "Six Picassos."

DARTMOUTH COLLEGE LIBRARY BULLETIN. "The Rose of the Infanta"; "Sky"; "Spring Binding."

Acknowledgments

THE DARTMOUTH QUARTERLY (*By permission of the Trustees of Dartmouth College*). "Cross Word-Puzzle"; "Night Creatures"; "Proud Parent"; "There's Hell, There's Darkness."

GREENSLEEVES (*By permission of the Trustees of Dartmouth College*). "Birth of a Saviour"; "I Made a Man of Cretan Clay"; "Next-to-Godliness."

HARPER'S MAGAZINE. "Elegy for an Engineer"; "The Husking"; "Men at Work"; "Poem from a Cage"; "That Time of Year"; "Yggdrasill."

HIP POCKET POEMS. "Advice to Skeptics"; "Episode with an Aphid."

THE HUDSON REVIEW. "Checkmate"; "Emanation"; "The Fall" ("All in a wind . . ."); "If it is true that creation is mindless . . ."; "The Print of Man."

THE KENYON REVIEW. "Now the Instructed Mind."

THE LADIES' HOME JOURNAL. "Lovesong for Young Oedipus"; "Words for a Boy."

THE LITERARY REVIEW (*Winter, 1966-1967; published by Fairleigh Dickinson University, Teaneck, N. J.*). "Age of Unreason"; "Aim"; "Alarm"; "Anthropoeides"; "Aquitation"; "Better Friend"; "Blessed Are the Poor in Taxco"; "The Chase of the Child"; "Cocklebread Song"; "Fall" (from Rilke); "Genetrix"; "God"; "Immediate Freedom"; "Manfight"; "Nature and Human History"; "Negroes of New Orleans"; "Nursery Rhyme"; "Pius Thought"; "The Place of the Merry-go-round"; "Prayer of an Ovulating Female"; "Protocol"; "Quest of Truth"; "Search"; "The Soul's House"; "Statics of Composition"; "Who Is Not Who"; "Veterans."

McCALL'S. "Second Expulsion."

THE MASSACHUSETTS REVIEW (© 1960, *The Massachusetts Review, Inc.*). "Night Creatures"; "Scape-Grace"; "Venus Petrified."

THE NATION. "And Goe the Fooles Among"; "Anti-Poem"; "Aubade"; "Big Toy"; "The City and the Song"; "The Compassionate Torturers"; "The Dazzled Ones"; "Don't Tread on Us"; "The Double Goer"; "I Attend a Reception for a Visiting Celebrity"; "Ignis Dominae"; "In a Green Shade"; "Let Them Ask Their Husbands"; "Maintenant"; "The Pure Passion"; "Six Picassos"; "Song After Seven Glasses of Picasso"; "Threnody on the Demise of As and Now"; "Walled City"; "We Who Are Civilized Salute Ourselves"; "Weddings and Banquets."

THE NEW LEADER. "Debris"; "F.F.V."; "The Help Is in You."

THE NEW MASSES. "Great and Small"; "Maidanek, Dachau, Buchenwald."

THE NEW REPUBLIC. "Hegira."

THE NEW YORK HERALD TRIBUNE. "Love, without Love . . ."; "Time of Ruin."

Acknowledgments

THE NEW YORK TIMES (© 1962, 1963, 1964, 1966, 1967 by the New York Times Company. Reprinted by permission.). "Atlantic Inland"; "Compost Art"; "Excursion to the Goddess"; "The Good Children"; "The Natural-born"; "Pinwheel"; "Plan Ahead"; "Poem" ("The star watcher . . ."); "Ring Time"; "Song for a Nativity"; "Song for a Tribe"; "Yellowstone"; "Zero."

THE NEW YORKER. "Back Country"; "Cartoon for a Weaver"; "Cock Crow"; "Cuckoo, Jug, Jug, Pu We, To Witta Wool"; "Ego"; "Extrovert"; "Eye Strain"; "Gamine"; "Icarus in the White Mountains"; "Lines on the Sea"; "Lutesong for Young Angels"; "Monograph on the Grasshopper"; "New England Extract"; "New England Scrap Heap"; "November Abstract"; "Pattern on File"; "Romance"; "Sculptor"; "Small Elegy"; "Snow"; "Song for December"; "Ten Leagues Beyond the Wide World's End"; "To a Mathematician"; "Vermont Evening"; "Victorian Seraglio"; "The Village"; "Vive le Roi!"

PM. "Another England."

PALMS. "Quatrain"; "Time . . . and Springtime."

THE PHOENIX. "Afternoon Tea"; "De Profundis"; "The Eternal"; "The Maker"; "Nunc Dimittis."

POETRY. "Afternoon of a Fore-Thinker"; "Bell"; "Capsule Dragon"; "The Catch"; "Dance of Burros"; "Eros Out of the Sea"; "Flowers Out of Rock"; "Genesis and Exodus"; "Harsh Return"; "I Shall Know"; "Nautilus"; "Occult Adventure"; "Picasso's Candlefire"; "The Proud"; "Rescue"; "Root and Branch"; "Saint Giotto of Assisi"; "The Swift Ships"; "Time Is All a Year"; "To Dolores Preserved"; "The Uncreation"; "Welcome Song."

POETRY CHAP-BOOK. "The Answer"; "The Little Girls."

PRAIRIE SCHOONER. "Twenty Below" in "Two Cold Poems."

PRISMA. "Elegy for an Engineer," with a German translation by Ina Seidel; "Not One Atoll," with a German translation by Dora Lubach.

PROVIDENCE JOURNAL. "Drink-Me"; "Fugue in a Field"; "Migrants."

PUNCH. "Therapy."

THE QUARTERLY REVIEW OF LITERATURE. "The Apparition"; "Man in His New Dimension."

THE QUEST. "The Beautiful Lady without Choice"; "Conversation between the Curies"; "Druid"; "Epitaph"; "Harsh Trainer"; "Human Image"; "Landlocked"; "Letter to the Prioress from a Lay Sister"; "Now"; "Private Entry in the Diary of a Female Parent"; "Springclean"; "The Tenth Symphony"; "To the Importunate One."

THE REPORTER. "Bearing Gifts"; "Freshman"; "The Hero in Two Metals"; "How Many Days?"

vii

Acknowledgments

THE SATURDAY EVENING POST. "Blackout"; "Tree Toad"; "Two Prepositional Endings."

THE SATURDAY REVIEW. "Ballad of the Bright Hair"; "Cradle Cure"; "Easter"; "The Fall" ("At the world's end . . ."); "Funeral of Clocks"; "Grief of the Trojan Women"; "High Tide"; "Incorrupt"; "Love, without Love . . ."; "Matter of Fact"; "Mine, But Not to Keep"; "Native to That Place"; "Return to Strangeness"; "Round Song"; "The Sacred Wood"; "The Sheathed Anger"; "Sonnet to a Sister in Error"; "Spheres of Be and Do"; "Summer, Be Slow"; "Temperature"; "Transience of Pain"; "Tree of Fire"; "When Yellow Leaves . . ."; "The Wild Bird."

SNOWY EGRET. "Naturalist."

THEMA. "Men at Work."

TOMORROW. "Dimensional Rhyme."

THE TRANSATLANTIC REVIEW. "Report of the Dreamer."

THE TUFTONIAN. "Not One Atoll."

THE UNIVERSITY OF KANSAS CITY REVIEW. "Tenochtitlán of the Gods."

THE VALLEY NEWS. "Change"; "The Grove"; "Monstrous Issue"; "To David."

THE VIRGINIA QUARTERLY REVIEW. "Between"; "Creature"; "The Dilettantes"; "Dove"; "Explaining van Gogh"; "Form"; "Let Me Hold You Far"; "The Little Bright One"; "Losing Game"; "Metamorphosis of Rimbaud"; "Morning Grouch"; "Penalty of Excellence"; "The Poets"; "Prescription (Obsolete)"; "The Pull"; "To Members of a Holy Order."

VOICES. "Afternoon of a Grown-up"; "Fox of Fire"; "Gloria Mundi"; "Hemisphere"; "Intimate Apocalypse"; "Kwan Yin"; "Lamp"; "The Latest Puritan"; "Locked in Amber"; "New England"; "Photo Graph"; "The Tall Tower"; "Timber Crew"; "Vision of Peace."

WINGS. "Mirror Thought."

THE YALE REVIEW. "I, Adam"; "Love Has So Terrible a Face"; "Northwest."

THE YORKSHIRE POST. "I Made a Man of Cretan Clay."

Editorial Note

The arrangement of this collection reflects both the view Dilys Laing had of her own work and the sequential development of her art. *Poems from a Cage*, published after her death, comes first because she selected for it—in the last year of her life—the poems by which she wished to be known afresh after a decade of much writing but little publication. It was her own design that its typescript of 111 poems be compressed in consultation with her editors. This had to be done, as M. L. Rosenthal explains in his Introduction, without her veto, and therefore may have been done more severely than she would have wished. (If so, the poems omitted have now been brought between these covers.) Sixty-seven of the 111 which she had nominated were retained for the volume as originally published, and two others were added. One of these two, the poem that stands first, may have been the last that she wrote. It was found in her briefcase in the room in which she died. One section of *Poems from a Cage* has been omitted in this reprinting because it contains 18 poems from the poet's earlier books, all three of which are here offered in full: *Another England* (1941), *Birth Is Farewell* (1944), and *Walk Through Two Landscapes* (1949). This sequence reveals the poet's contemporary estimate of her accomplishment throughout the decade of her emergence as a writer of consequence.

For the second half of the present volume, some of Dilys's friends, aided by two editors capable of objectivity because they had never met her, selected about half of the poems found in manuscript after her death. They also chose 45 poems from the 63—published in periodicals during her lifetime—that do not appear in the earlier books. She may have meant to abandon some of these, when she withdrew them deliberately from her first three typescripts; but she may, as well, have been reserving them for later use because each of her books had a thematic arrangement. Early in the 1950's she was assembling a manuscript for a book to be called *Beasts and Fables,* a title given after her death to a group of 15 poems published in the *Virginia Quarterly Review.* Her own typescript of *Beasts and Fables* had included some poems withdrawn from *Walk Through Two Landscapes.*

To test my own estimate of the merits of Dilys's unpublished poetry I began soon after her death to offer manuscripts to the periodicals I knew she had respected. One hundred sixty poems have appeared in print since then, more than two-thirds of them in journals that value verse at least enough to pay for it. All of the poems that had appeared in national magazines at any time, from 1928 to the present, were included in the initial typescript of this volume. In the final choice, 25 of those published after the poet's death were withdrawn. Thus 43 poems, published in periodicals during or after the poet's lifetime, have been left out. One reason for recording the total is that many of these are topical light verse, an aspect of Dilys's interest which survives in this collection with something less than a fair proportionate representation.

I have tried to date all of the poems. Those in the second half of this book have an approximate chronological sequence, beginning with a small sampling of the abundant early work. Whenever a date appears on a manuscript it has been given exactly. Most dates were established by an examination of correspondence with editors or from entries in Dilys's extensive journals, in which some early drafts appear. If no close evidence has been found, a poem published in the poet's lifetime usually has been dated in the year prior to its first printing. Watermarks and topical references also have been helpful. Most of the poems were products of intensive work during a period of several days, but many were in a process of revision over months or years; the limiting dates, when they are evident in such cases, have been given.

A large division, and an important one, occurs at the point in the autumn of 1951 when she dropped from her professional signature the middle name—Bennett—that appears on the title pages of all her books except the posthumous one. The choice was carefully arrived at (as letters to Mrs. E. B. White, John Ciardi, and others attest); all her published work and all her signed manuscripts thereafter carry the shorter form of the name. The fact is helpful in roughly dating some poems that have no other indication of the time of their composition. What is much more important, the decision was a part of Dilys's conscious shift in subject matter and style, at this time, which she also discusses in letters and in her journal. The shift was evolutionary, without a sharp beginning or completion, but its general nature will be evident to the critical reader.

Throughout her creative life Dilys typically submitted her work to the judgment of her friends. She was both grateful and gracious to her critics. For example, she circulated a tentative typescript of *Birth Is Farewell* among advisers who included the Philip Wheelwrights, collecting such notes as this one:

> Maude liked this better than P. The last ten lines
> pack a terrifying accusation, but the first four seem
> misleading—as if the images to come were created
> out of the brain—i.e., the emphasis is too subjective
> for the realism of the sequel.

The poem was "Guilt." In the margin Dilys has written, "First four lines deleted."

The Collected Poems of Dilys Laing owes its existence in this form to friends and advisers who happened to be most available when most needed. Ramon Guthrie and Howard Webber have read and evaluated all of the poems which seemed to me to have been completed according to the poet's own usual standards of craftsmanship. David Hartwell brought back into consideration 36 poems from a group of nearly two hundred which I had tentatively set aside for various reasons of detail. Twenty-five of these 36 were approved by the other advisers and have been included. Thomas and Vera Vance have aided in the selection of poems, and with the galleys, which also were read by Eve Bennett, Dilys's

xi

Editorial Note

mother, who supplied holographs, biographical information, and dates. Reed Whittemore contributed greatly to the revival of interest in Dilys's work by publishing the first large group of 27 newly found poems in 1963, in *The Carleton Miscellany*. The nature of M. L. Rosenthal's contribution should be evident from his Introduction. It was he who produced the beginnings of this renaissance when he encouraged Dilys to submit work to *The Nation* in the last two or three years of her life, and then arranged for the publication by Macmillan of *Poems from a Cage*. Geraldine Jacobson gave me early and invaluable aid in sorting and recording a chaotic mass of manuscripts. She and her husband, Nicholas Jacobson, stand with their love behind this book. It is hard to stop naming because it was a quality of Dilys, as an artist, that she drew others into the orbit of her artistry to mutual advantage. The name of Richard Eberhart occurs again and again in her journals as she picks up, wherever they had left it, their running argument over prosody. I must mention Richmond Lattimore's poem for his dead friends, with its line, "Dilys, who was delight." To stand for many others who have testified in a variety of ways, there are, finally, the dedications "To Dilys" in books of poems by Ramon Guthrie, Bink Noll, and Frederic Will.

ALEXANDER LAING

Introduction

Although Dilys Laing was not famous, many other poets admired her work. There were always people who recognized her quality. Three books of her poetry appeared in her lifetime; the fourth and best, *Poems from a Cage* (1961), appeared a year after her death at the age of fifty-three. With her husband, the poet Alexander Laing, and with their old friend and neighbor, the poet Ramon Guthrie, I shared the pleasure and the pain of editing that posthumous volume.

It was then that I first experienced one of the most shocking of artistic realities—that a poet's voice comes most piercingly to life in his work after his literal voice is unrecallable. Dilys had been a beloved friend. Her poems had always won me, and I had published a number of them when I was poetry editor of *The Nation* and had encouraged her to get the fourth book together after ten years of "silence." Yet now the purity, the compassion, the suffering, the vividness came through as never before. I understood in a new way how *human* the true poetic voice is, how gallantly it stands out against all that is precarious and brutal and dooming in life. The slightest effects, if they are the real thing, can stop the heart for a moment, as when Dilys sings so debonairly of her own coming death at the beginning of "To David":

> When I go to the Capital
> where I dream of going. . . .

In "Transience of Pain," a poem that came to her while she was "listening to Rudolf Serkin," we can see in cameo the precise structure of her spirit against a background of half dream-reverie. An image of the human predicament arises, summoned up by the music and endlessly relevant. The poem is at once clear in its realism and psychologically accurate in its projection of both the passionate need for solutions and the elusiveness of the exact source of that need. All this is complex enough, yet the poem makes everything simple. It is the *grief* in the voice that does it:

> It happens and unhappens
> in the recording cortex:
> structures of love and
> images of suffering
> rise and resolve

> Wounded fawn in the thicket
> I must go to him I must go
> Antlers caught in the branches
> I cannot bear his terror
> I must go to him and I go
> but there are no antlers
> there is no fawn

One more instance—the first and last stanzas of "Emanation," so apt to the particular point I am making now. Here Dilys, with her implicit poet's belief in the literal magic of language, projects the most poignantly modest modulation toward immortality that I know of:

> The poet sweats to build himself a ghost
> of words to haunt the world with, lest he be lost
> out of the mind of men with his own dust. . . .

> Stay, my ghost, and claim a slender space
> amongst these others. Sleep, my dust, in peace,
> if my words breathe an hour above the grass.

These elegiac recognitions and, in "Transience of Pain," the cruel confrontation of the conscientious and loving self with the elusiveness of its task when seeking to undo the tragic are made with the most economical, unpretentious immediacy. There is nothing extreme about Dilys's work. It *is* personal; it reveals a vulnerable sensibility. But though, at times, it approaches the confessional, and perhaps even the suicidal, it is never exhibitionistic. Nor, accomplished and versatile as it is, does it make a show of being drastically experimental. I have often paid close and respectful attention to violent or extremist writing, as Dilys did too. Wonderful, powerful things have been done in these modes, especially in our time.

Introduction

But one must always remember the persistence of the clear lyric tradition, its way of working through some of the finest spirits by drawing flame from their intensity and honesty of feeling and from their sheer intrinsic pressure to be directly articulate. We shall never be sure that when the "siftings on siftings in oblivion" are completed it will not be their writings alone that will remain. On this subject, a friend wrote me recently that "people are missing the point of this time. What is wanted is not experiment, and extensions of experience. . . . If technology and all that means anything, doesn't it really mean that the centuries of experiment are over and that now we have to face the fact of choice—choice of world, choice of what man is to be—a situation which doesn't call for 'experiment' at all, but rather something much more ethical . . .?" In the prevailing current view, he says, "even the Death Camps come to seem a kind of 'good' because they seem more profound or 'interesting'—deeper—than had been suspected. And poetry becomes something of the same sort. . . . I want to ask, what is the value of this kind of depth, or isn't there another kind of depth . . .?"

I am far from agreeing with some of the assumptions behind my friend's thoughts, but they are most provocative. If there is "another kind of depth" to be taken into account, I do think it is represented by Dilys Laing. Hers is not an alternative, in my way of thinking, to the dangerous exploration of man's repressed nature and to the formal aspects of that exploration. Rather, it goes side by side with it, a lyrical correlative. Dilys's chief talent was to write beautifully and simply, with ardor, candor, wit. But the reader will see in poem after poem—for instance, in "In Horror of History"—that the dark psychological and historical depths of man are her subject as well as Robert Lowell's or Charles Olson's:

> In horror of history
> the reading spirit shuts the book of wounds
> wakes from the dungeon dream. . . .
>
> In horror of history
> the reasoning angel shuts the book of wars
> begs an eighth day of God.

Introduction

She can be bitter, though never with the bile of life-hatred. Humor and humanism combine with imagination to save her from that fate. Thus, she is a feminist, but of the most *womanly* kind. Old-fashioned militant feminists had their points, and Dilys shared their uncompromising refusal to accept second place in the human universe. Coming upon St. Paul's admonition in I Corinthians 14:35 ("And if they will learn anything let them ask their husbands at home: for it is a shame for women to speak in the church"), she descanted wryly on one of her favorite ideas—that God is *female*. In "Let Them Ask Their Husbands," she writes:

> In human need
> of the familiar
> I see God
> woman-shaped
>
> for God created
> woman in Her own image
> and I have
> my Pauline pride.

Political tendentiousness is likely to be humorless, most of all where self-irony is involved, and so I am not sure whether any of the noble heroines of women's rights would have found this poem as amusing, or its first two lines as charmingly self-corrective, as we can today. The poem "Villanelle," with its frank tribute to male sexuality, certainly marks an advance in the feminine right of self-expression that would have shocked those ladies if they could have believed what they were reading. There never was any stridency in Dilys's work, but there was very often a clean accuracy buoyed up by her love of high-spirited speech and of sound for its own sake:

> Proud inclination of the flesh
> most upright tendency, salute
> in honor of the secret wish.
>
> Slant attitude. When anglers fish
> they hold their rods in this acute
> proud inclination of the flesh. . . .

The thought, *naturally*, is a woman's. The skill and exuberance, however, are neither masculine nor feminine but human.

Introduction

They are alive, of the very essence of the poetic. Merely gross language, the shortcut that semipoets occasionally take to sensual expression, would have been impossible to such a writer. It might have been adequate as the self-expression of a pornographically oriented mind, but not as that of a person speaking out of the whole complex of subtle perceptiveness and resourceful artistry as well as of responsive desire that "Villanelle" distills. The person speaking is the same who at the beginning of "Aubade" can say:

> My bed rocks me gently
> in the pale shallows
> of 5 A.M.

And at the end:

> The great light of morning
> shines and shakes
> in my eyes.

That is, the most important organs are the delighted ear and eye. All feeling must come to us by way of them. A classical devotion to her art went hand in hand with Dilys Laing's classical tough-mindedness. "When I say exactly what I think," she once observed to me, "people always think I'm joking." Essential truthfulness is always unexpected—that is half the character of classical wit.

On the other hand, hers is not the dry classicism of an Yvor Winters or a J. V. Cunningham. She is closer to the Sapphic tradition, that aspect of the pure lyric stream as we follow it through figures as varied as Catullus, Villon, Emily Dickinson, and the Pound outside the *Cantos* and of moments within them. This is of course a great poetic tradition. However, far more meaningful than the question of whether we are to call her "great" is the fact that Dilys Laing was a genuine poet who thought as a poet and respected her art and loved and stood in awe of it. When I speak of her as in the Sapphic tradition I am thinking of a disciplined lyricism in which there is no fear of passion, no *necessary* anti-Romanticism, but on the contrary a deep charge of feeling. The classical aspect is mainly embodied in her power of suggestive concentration,

Introduction

her reluctance to let go in mere expansiveness and self-indulgence.

But if there is no fear of feeling in this poet, there is by the same token no fear of intellect either. Gentle, pitying, passionately alert as she was in every private personal sense, she also brings abstract intelligence into play in her writing, and certain very strongly humane political and social concerns. The intelligence is modern—desperate over war and injustice, appalled by poverty, inclined toward that necessary set of openness to revolutionary possibility (but without dogmatism of any kind) that is indispensable if man is to survive the age and still remain man. In this respect she shares the anguish of such poets as Lowell and Sylvia Plath, though never going all out for the sheer power that the absolute release of such anguish can lead to, for it leads to loss of psychological self-control as well and is in danger of becoming too dependent on that which nourishes the destructive principle. In Dilys Laing's poems, too, we see a questioning modern intelligence combined with a genuine religious instinct. She returns again and again to Biblical notes, theological questions, figures of angels, visions, quarrels with God and with her own conscience. Aztec life and religion fascinated her imagination, as some of the poems show and as her friends know from her plans to make deeper poetic studies of that civilization. So much of this many-sided person makes itself manifest in her writings that we can well say that here was a poet who brought the whole of life into her work—and that life includes marriage and motherhood as well as all the other motifs I have noted. The poems are rich with that personal reality which only an art impersonal in its discipline can realize. A familiar principle, admittedly, but surely the poems here collected reveal its validity in a fresh and special way.

M. L. Rosenthal

Suffern, N. Y.

May, 1967

xviii

Contents

Poems from a Cage (1961)

Contents

II. TRANSLATIONS

Contents

Another England (1941)

I

II

III

Contents

Birth Is Farewell (1944)

Contents

Contents

Walk Through Two Landscapes (1949)

Contents

Previously Uncollected Poems: 1921-1951

Contents

Contents

Contents

Previously Uncollected Poems: 1951-1960

Contents

Contents

Contents

Translations Not Previously Collected

Poems
from
a Cage

1961

For

Alexander Laing
Ramon Guthrie
M. L. Rosenthal

IN SUBMITTING HER MANUSCRIPT, the poet wrote:
"I owe to Philip Booth the title of the first poem
which gives its name to the whole. There are
other poems here in which the idea of a cage, or
of captivity, is paramount, as well as poems of
release. They celebrate two conditions basic to
poetry as to life. I am indebted to Jacques Prévert
for his kind permission to include my translations
from his book *Paroles*, published by the Librairie
Gallimard, Le Point du Jour, N.R.F."

To David

When I go to the Capital
where I dream of going
I shall take with me
very little luggage

Neither my feet nor hands
neither my eyes nor ears
nor yet the bright blood
the clear lymph nor the built bones

But I shall pack and take,
traveling so lightly,
memories of Mozart,
and of your violin

singing under your fingers
and of your eyes shining
with the music's light:
that jewel I'll smuggle.

Late 1959

I

Poem from a Cage

Between the lion cage and the antelope cage
I found the angel cage.
There a fine specimen of Homo pneumaticus
with great fullfeathered wings and empty eyes
huddled in a corner, the wings folded about it
like a pair of silver dishes.
I threw it a peanut and snapped my fingers at it in a friendly way.

Here Angel! Nice Angel!
But it turned to me its terrible void eyes
and I knew that my image did not fall into those pupils
which nevertheless were not blind
but saw another thing by another light.
Feeling with surprise the key to the cage in my hand
I unlocked the door.
Go—poor creature!
The angel departed in a thunder of wings and robes.

The gate clanged.

The cage encloses me like ribs.
Where is the key I turned to set the angel
free from a cockeyed clockwork zoo?
Lion and antelope look in
at Homo ridiculus trying to pick the lock
with this cut quill snatched from escaping wings.

January–February 3, 1952

The City and the Song

Metronomes deafen the musicians
The ears of the learned are dull with discourse
The mechanical city ticks like a bomb
In the desert outside the walls the beloved lies bound
Anointed with honey and tortured by ants, he sings
Only the loving can measure the song with their pulses as, listening
for it, they twist the dials of time
The song ends. The city sickens
Barometers on the walls of the oblivious fall with the silence and
weathermen forecast frost
A stranger short of breath cries news of the hill of bones outside the
walls
and ephemeral columns print eternal news

The city of ants is dead. The singing youth was old, is dead. The ribs
that sang are filled with roots
A truth grows from the bones—a tree whose leaves aim at infinity and
find the mercy of limits
Circle this hill of pain. Drink at its brook
Under the singing tree, above the bones, gather flowers amazing as
the questions of children

1952–April, 1959

The Grove

Trees of the grove lean all one way
in a green parliament of leaves
agreeing with the air

The moon, our constant waterclock,
measures the future with the past
and time is in the hand

The ribboned membranes of the grass
shudder but do not bend. The wind
flows from an ancient night

The loved and loving are together
with human intellect and vision
to read and work the spell

Once, grain was goddess, god was light,
and men and women charged with grace
rendered the ritual word

Now hemlock willow birch and elm
like holy sisters—nuns or dryads—
signal past the eye

and past the ear the frogs declare
a credo of desire, a power
of passion over death

Nothing has changed. When faith is tenant
the resurrecting year provides
circumference for love

1956-58

(See "Maintenant," page 395.)

Time Is All a Year

The wide eye in the mind
can see between the snow
its yesterday of sail
seabird and shell and wet
          and all a sky alight

Salt sandshine and the rush
of sky among the shell
and the tern's sandy egg
on the egg-colored sand
          and sand is all afire

The sharp ear in the mind
here in the inland air
catches the pitch of surf
the thin tone of the tern
          and air is all a tune

sky's shellshout and the groan
of fog, the mandoom waves
smacking the herring hulls
the gulls that laugh for bread
          and food is all a cry

Summer done and to do
known sea, again to know,
wide angle of a lens
catching a whole horizon
          and time is all a year

1950

Night Creatures

Bestial innocence illumines my dream.
Out of the reticence of thickets
torches shine
that are the eyes of watchfulness
awaiting love

They who await love expect treachery.
Fright is in them like music
teasing their fibres.
They who desire so much have room in them
for piteous loss

And so they turn and turn on moonlit feet
fold themselves sadly to their beds of leaf
and quiver into sleep

1952

Song After Seven Glasses of Picasso

For Ramon Guthrie

A woman made of wire
and double mirrors
and distances

I make a sonata
for the idea
of the woman

A man made of boxes
and bulls and
passages

I make a cantata
for the idea
of the man

A peace made of tanks
after a battle
of doves

I make a canon
for the idea
of peace

BUT

the wire woman
and the cubic man
can marry in an orbit
of virginals
and have a child
in green sharp minor

I ring a gong
for the probability
of the impossible

Early 1952

To Dolores Preserved

Lured and repelled, the natural history class
pauses (just past the lizard and the ape)
to see you standing in your box of glass
stark in the remnant of your human shape:
bones in a bag of parchment, shrunken head,
eyeless toothless and gaping, and your hair
looking, Dolores, most like what it was
once, when you combed it with a living care
to catch the sun, or loose it for the night

Body of blindness! Long ago the light
rang in your skull its paradisal chime,
promising everything of beauty and love,
never this glass through which the curious gaze
frightening reason with the price of time

Life is a welfare not to waste or lose,
sweet as a fruit to nourish infinite days.
And yet I know, Dolores, as I look
aghast and grieved at all this leather and hair
dusty and dreadful in this sunless nook
more pitiless and public than the grave,
you are the portrait of the mind's despair,
you are the ash of all I make or choose

Now you have time for death and I have none,
and I have time for love and yours is spent.
I do not wish to watch you, but I must.
Now shrive me with your image. Let me save
out of the dread of your archival dust
the means, for my remainder of the sun,
for all the kindness I have ever meant

Spring, 1951

Hegira

The swarming scarabs of the mind
gather to form their ritual rings.
I study but have not divined
the hieroglyphics of their feet.
Before their meaning is defined,
while still their rounds are incomplete,
the beetles dart on sudden wings
sunward. I watch them and go blind.

1954

I Attend a Reception
for a Visiting Celebrity

Everyone clamoring
with tongue so clever
my own tongue
is struck to the root.
I shrink my telescopes
into my shell
delicately retract my slimy tail
and parody a pebble.
The lion roars.
The sheep pull their own wool
over their own eyes
and the wolves fawn.
And in my shell cell
by my sole self
modest
unassuming
and seething with pride
I turn on my tape recorder

1958 (?)

Dance of Burros

Nothing at all more delicate and charming
than the way the donkeys came,
their eyes downcast like eyes of señoritas
taught to dissemble shame

their small hooves treading neatly, shoes of dancers
making a shape for music, striking the stones
into sudden tune, tapping the brookbed street
to echo on the adobe. How could bones

travel so nimbly under the tall sun
carrying burdens as the donkeys did:
cubed fields of cornstalks? And the pale maize rustled
in frail percussion from the carrying tread.

Piano piano piano the beasts drummed by
with delicate beat, as light as twigs on tile,
through raining light above their own small shadows
trotting in single file.

And three brown men in white, beneath sombreros,
moved with the donkeys quietly, to climb
the cobbled hill. The white walls yawned them in,
burros and men and burdens keeping time.

March, 1951

Lost, Stolen, Strayed

The gone dog leaves a ghost.
His bark comes to the door.
Running against our knowing
we whistle to a wish

We hear his shaking ears
and see the birch at the window
shiver. It was a bird
that fluttered sudden wings

Returning home, we see
solid delusive air
wagging a welcome dance
baring teeth in a smile

He was so very here.
Now through the hills of where
he runs—and wounds our waiting
with shams of his return

July 29, 1955

The Sacred Wood

FOR NED O'GORMAN

In the forest of the Alphabet the child
could not pass the tree called Fear.
    The deathly owls came mewing from its boughs
    and ripped the hinges of his tongue.

    The boy wept at his teacher's knee:
    "I cannot learn to read my life."

In the forest of the Alphabet the youth
could not pass the tree called Joy.
    Two phoenixes came flying from its boughs
    and tried to strike his tongue to fire.

    The youth said to the long-eared crowd:
    "Your eyes have stricken me with fear,
    I cannot read my poems clear."

In the forest of the Alphabet the man
reached the holy oak Omega.
    The winged sun was beating in its boughs
    and dropped a leaf of light upon his tongue.

    The poet sang to the black century:
    "Here in the sacred wood I stand,
    a sickle burning in my hand
    to cut the bough that is a brand,
    and they who love will understand."

1956

Two Cold Poems

I. TEN BELOW

Sniffing the news, the spaniel bitch
swims before me on her snowplow paws
through air from which quicksilver shrinks.
Her breath is an epiphany. She smokes
like a Chinese dragon. Her ears are wings
that swoop to quest the scribbled kerb.

On harpstring leather with a right good will
she tugs me through the swordbright noon.
Not she, but just her left hind foot
suddenly learns how cold it is
and she becomes a tripod dog,
a mild and tiny lion of Jerome
with prickled paw. But still she snuffles on
(suffering martyrdom with half her heed)
to analyze the yellow snow.

II. TWENTY BELOW

Time to put out the cats. They twitch their feet,
flinch and huddle and reproach the door
with eyes like aching emeralds.
In pity we recall them. They flow back,
forgiven souls to resurrection,
and find their corners
and curl in hoops of sleep.

We drink our rye. The spent log breaks
in fiery crumbs. We yawn and climb to bed.
A bigger cat than all, the furnace purrs
and mocks the humming cold.
Under our blanket woven with charged wires,
locked in our mutual mortal warmth,

we think askance of creeping polar caps.

All night long the cable-tethered house
drifts like a sloop moored to a telephone pole.
The G string wires moan through our hindered sleep;
the beams, contracting, bang away like cannons.

January 15, 1957

Afternoon of a Fore-Thinker

The rock was hard behind my back
    hard as thought and hard as bone
    the sky enclosed me like a brain
and the sea burned like a wick

the sea burned and the seabirds flew
    as sparks above the spinning flame.
    The dark rock shook. I took my name
and flung it at the thinking sky

and the sky gave me nothing back
    no wink no word no code no sign
    the seabirds rose with beaks of pain
and nailed my mind upon the rock

1950

Profane Witness

"Hosannah to the beasts!" the angels cried.
"Praise them who by man's hands are crucified
for meat and leather, ivory and oil.
Bless them whom men call spoil.
Praise to their patience, courtesy, and trust.
Since men won't praise them, God's own angels must!"

I stood among the singers, and I tried
not to look human, opened my mouth wide
and sang, though scarcely as an angel sings,
hunched up my shoulders to resemble wings,
pushed my hat backwards, praying that the brim
looked like the haloes of the seraphim.

Useless. The angels smelt me, turned about
and pointed at me, till I dwindled out.

On hands and knees I left, but not before
I'd heard a lion from the altar roar
and twenty elephants from twenty trunks
blare TE LEONEM like Gregorian monks.
Rising, I peered a moment from the porch
and saw the whole nave blazing like a torch.
The music ended. All was hushed because
of the laying on of huge angelic paws.

Early 1953

Saint Giotto of Assisi

FOR RAMON GUTHRIE

Dismounted Mercy holds his molten cloak
across the picture to the humbled bankrupt,
bestows his golden alms forever
with a gesture free and gentle.

Six centuries the horse stands by
and nibbles at the abstract rock.
The toyblock church and isometric town
hang counterweighted on their backdrop hills.

Trees like dusty corals struggle from stone.
Nature and conscience make a cross in man,
whose handwrought halo wedlocks earth and sky.
The beggar bows, eternally enriched.

My wall exclaims with color cameracaught
from an Umbrian wall. The visionary shepherd
makes me this gift of parable and pigment,
this liberal mantle for a meagre time.

1949–53

Aubade

My bed rocks me gently
in the pale shallows
of 5 A.M.

Lying beside you I wait
for the tree-toad clock-bell
to scream you awake

My ears are full of trees
in which choruses of birds
explode

The great light of morning
shines and shakes
in my eyes

1958 (?)

Villanelle

Proud inclination of the flesh,
most upright tendency, salute
in honor of the secret wish.

Slant attitude. When anglers fish
they hold their rods in this acute
proud inclination of the flesh

as purely in the waters thrash
the living fish like silver fruit
in honor of the secret wish.

For who's so risky or so rash
he would forbid this absolute
proud inclination of the flesh?

No woman, truly. Let her blush
and hide her thoughts. Herself she'll suit
in honor of the secret wish.

Let scholars all their reasons thresh—
this argument they'll not refute:
proud inclination of the flesh
in honor of the secret wish.

Fall, 1957

Tenochtitlán of the Gods

Through castling hills we came, and the Plumed Serpent
became a road to wind us to the central city.
We put this strangeness between us and our meadows:
these violet steeps of ancient death and beauty
under the buzzard squadrons, where the human hills
cry with bones. The mesas are not mountains,
but pyramids where the old gods were killed
to irrigate a crop of Spanish priests.

And we came at last to the great Tenochtitlán,
to "the place where cactus grows out of the stone."
The fair valley of knowledge assuaged the mind
with wisdom of plowing done to catch the sky,
with dark jade fences of maguey, and palms,
and palaces of art which house the poor
in furious pigment: the intellectual peasant
snapping his chains. And in the city of Tenochtitlán
we found the actual huts where in the dust
the Aztec seed bursts feebly in flowers of defeat.

We said then with disappointment, turning aside with tears:
Tenochtitlán is everywhere. And we are there.
We've come a circling way, back to the starting place,
the hub central to the four distances and to the four chambers
        of the heart,
the old valley of the gods where all the gods are killed,
where every idol is betrayed by him who built it high,
where the great leave their lonely names upon a lapsing wind,
and only the little poor live forever.

Spring, 1951–early 1953

Transience of Pain

Poem while Listening to Rudolf Serkin

It happens and unhappens
in the recording cortex:
structures of love and
images of suffering
rise and resolve

Wounded fawn in the thicket
I must go to him I must go
Antlers caught in the branches
I cannot bear his terror
I must go to him and I go
but there are no antlers
there is no fawn

1957 (?)

Dream Between Sleeps

The wood swims out of the sea   A cockerel bell
wakes me to listen to the lizards call
madly   and fine in feathers   among leaves

Who imagined birds?   Who had this happy plan
to make a reptile fly   fish crawl from waves
a boneless sea-urge find itself a spine
a planet scarf itself with sea   a sun
fling off a whirling drop of liquid fire
a darkness kindle at its core a star?

Wingéd amphibians flit from tree to tree

The sea is restless with the seeds of shape
the sea is filled with sleep

                    and I

                              with sleep

with sleep   with dragons
                         the wood slides under the sea.

1949–July, 1953

Scape-Grace

Into the stone asylum of the terrace
he pours his grassy braid out of the light.
The jade greaves of his walking belly shiver with his heart

Safe in the placid muscular embrace of his twined kin
he slides and hides his spatulate bright head
till fear of brandished hate subsides

He sleeps. And wakes. Hunts meat and mate
and glimmers in the uncut outer grass, assuming
the shape of evil for the evil eye

Summer, 1952

Advice to Skeptics

Bend
  down
    and
pick a waterlily
    out
   of
  the
summer sky

1959 (?)

I Shall Know

I shall know that leafless landscape when I reach it,
with its drought and barrenness, its lack of promises.
I shall know it for what it is
and ask no more of it—that bitterness so long expected—
where all is solitary and without deception,
and in the black rock and the icy wind
I shall discover forever my own absence.

1952 (?)—September 28, 1953

The Pure Passion

The wind has hollowed me.
All that remains
is sister to the stones
wife to the sky

On quartz-bright rock
hot from daylong sun
I feel the bones and vigor
of the world

Life beats in the lake
as in my veins.
My vision thrusts to sand
bent by gold water

Green-listening pines
slant waterwards, reflect
into my eyes
my look of wakened love

Early 1958

Smoking Mirror

"Sick of a heart disease whose only cure is gold"
Christ's mercenary soldiers are abroad
They've staked their hangman's cross at the world's selvage
foundered their ships behind them
and burst like curses from God's mouth on Satan's kingdom

I

The morning star smokes in the greenstone sky

The priestking's augurs, wailing, bring a bird
with a mirror in its head. The king sees in the glass
an armed host snaking from his fronded coast
up to his city of reflecting fires

His eyes are caved with shadow. What is sleep?
A woman's voice has mourned through meteored nights—
maternal dirge of the Snake Ancestress:

"My children! We are lost. Where can I lead you?"
Death in the mirror, death in the star, and in the voice
death for Tenochtitlán and Moctezuma

What in the face of prophecy but acquiescence?
When God claims sacrifice the mind assents

Welcome, predicted warriors—God-promised gods!
Your burdenbeasts have hair like that of maidens
Your lolltongued hounds flow by like waves that drown

Pour upon us as it was foretold
while on Tepeacac, the Hill of Reeds,
our Serpent Mother of the Maize rattles her staff
summoning from the cloud not rain but tears

The king who for God's feeding gathers hearts
feels his own heart, like his own fate, contract
Surely these maned men wear the battledress
of Huitzilopochtli? The anxious emperor sends
a lordly embassy to bear them as their due
plaques of the sun and moon, the plumes of Quetzalcoatl

He sends them also food most fit for gods:
eggplants and melons, quails and chocolatl
and bread of maize sprinkled with human blood
Strange how they shrink with loathing from the sacred bread
and take the unblest food with relish!

II

Manbeasts—men and horses saddlegrafted—
look to obsidian eyes like a new species
Manbeasts or godmen armed with metal reeds
that utter noise and fire to shock and kill
welcome the legates of the godstruck emperor
and feast their whetted eyes on fabulous gifts
of robes and greenstones and medicinal gold

III

Scouts bring proof that kindles a new hope:
these gods, the king learns, die of arrowwounds
and bleed like men
                          He sends his sorcerers
to smite the host with spells of fear and sickness

The necromancers meet a blackskinned stranger
who staggers in a drunken exaltation
and blasts at them with a hot wind of words:
"Go home! Go home! And hope no more for help from me
Does Moctezuma feel at last the horror of his crimes?
There has been too much death of men in Mexico

and for that sin—more death
                    Go from my sight
I have done with you now and forever

His fury is a wall they cannot breach
Homebound, they argue: "That was not a man
reeling with octli, but the black Tezcatlipoca
drunk with time's knowledge got from gazing
into the smoking mirror at his brow"

   IV

With her tongue Malintzin, lovestruck maiden,
born luckless in the sign of twisted grass,
sells her people for the conqueror's bed
and must spend time's remnant weeping among the hills
atoning with the voice of revolution

The swords of courteous Cortés cut off the hundred hands
of fifty captives—an offering to his god
And towns fall yielding slaves lives booty vassals hosts and glory
for Christ and Cortés and the King of Spain

   V

Greetings, deathbearer! The heart of Moctezuma
is a precious plume, a sapphire sungift
for the killed gods of the Tenochca

"The Feathered Serpent shall return
out of the East." This was the prophecy
You came—not gods—but hard blind men of greed
and have destroyed the world

Let the sun fall a fifth time flaming
down to Mictlampa of the shades and never rise again
squired from East to Zenith by chanting warriors,
from Zenith to the West by birthkilled women

Let heaven no longer shake with shields and singing
but let the obsidian gods roll down in thundering lava
between the smoldering jaws of the earthbeast Cipactli

while in raw churches hatched upon broken temples
the killed god of the victors weeps his blood
above the place where victims' hearts lay steaming—
victim among the victims, flesh and blood
consumed—a fantasy of sacrifice

But where Our Mother, Serpent Woman, stood
armed with the rain upon the Hill of Reeds,
Goddess of Battles, Mother of the Lightning,
she burns again on the reflecting air:
brown Virgin of the Conquest cloaked with stars

A mirror for the sorrow of Malintzin,
she smiles aslant at the obsidian people,
the maize people reaped by Toledo blades
that could not quench the gold fire of the corn

October, 1955

33

NOTES TO "SMOKING MIRROR"

Smoking Mirror: The symbol of prophecy shown in many of the codices as worn by Tezcatlipoca, the great obsidian god of life and death.

"Sick of a heart disease . . .": Cortés quoted by Gómara.

Snake Ancestress: Ciuacoatl, or Snake Woman, called Tonantzin, or Our Mother—a maize goddess, mother of gods and men.

Tenochtitlán: The "city of reflected fires," the capital of Moctezuma, built on an island and on reclaimed land in the Lake of Tezcuco. Fires burned perpetually on its temple tops.

Tepeacac: Reed Hill, present site of the Basilica of Guadalupe.

Huitzilopochtli: Aztec god of war.

Octli: Aztec word for pulque, fermented juice of the maguey, or aloe.

Malintzin: Or Marina, mistress of Cortés, and his interpreter. She is supposed to lend her spirit to revolutions in atonement for her betrayal of her people.

Feathered Serpent: Quetzalcoatl, the Toltec Prometheus, adopted by the Aztecs.

Mictlampa: Hades, or the land of the dead.

Valiant women: Women dead in childbirth accompanied Tonatiuh, the Sun, on the second half of his daily journey through heaven.

Virgin of the Conquest: Guadalupe, here identified with Malintzin and Ciuacoatl, mother of the gods.

Six Picassos

I

The mother is a pair of wings
that wish around the child

II

Circling the puzzled boy with fleshless arms
the old man starves and dreams

III

The naked ones embrace and thrust their darkness
into each other's kindled nerves

IV

An antique woman sits
and stares at God

V

A vitreous girl regards herself
in mirrors and time sings

VI

A dove of light
is written in the air

April 19–21, 1952

Venus Petrified

All the windows are shining. A great waltz flows
out of the house into the breathing dark.
Dancers come through a casement door that throws
a rhomb of honey onto indigo grass.
By twos they move among the elms and pines,
secret as deer evasive in a park.

The house, that seems a vessel blown in glass,
a phantom dwelling held erect by vines,
brims with a light the color of Moselle,
and high beyond the roof the meteors pour
like bright leaves scattering from a shaken bough
through black October.

                    Shallow tides of Strauss
swell to orgasmic oceans in my brain
and memory is a storm I can't repel.

Swept by the fury to go through that door
I try to move, but stand from foot to brow
rigid. My blood has run and left no stain.

I am that statue at the garden's end
which, crazed, and scarred with lichen, keeps the form
of Venus startled, hands poised to defend
what nothing threatens. I struggle to unbend
arms that the noonday sun can never warm.

The spilling windows blur and the whole house
flares, like a single star, with straws of light
and blinds me.

                 When the dark has healed my sight

the blood beats through my stone, and I discern
the old foundations bandaged thick with fern.

1957–59

Genesis and Exodus

The home that we all seek
is no man's land
between the right and the left hand
between the light and dark.

Woman and man, earth and heaven,
we face each other's garden
and find only Eden
from which we must be driven.

1945 (P)

The Double Goer

The woman took a train
away away from herself.
She thought: I need a change
and wheels make revolutions.
I'm half a century old
and must be getting somewhere.
And so she futured on
away from her own presence.

The landscape boiled around her
like a pan of beans.
A man without a face
made her ticket holy.
Adventure thrilled her nerves
restless rapture shook her.
Love is in the next seat,
she mused, and strength and glory
are over the hill, and I
grow younger as I leave
my me behind.

The telephone wires were staves
of a quintet score.
The hills were modulations
through the circle of keys.
Freedom is music, she thought,
smiling at the conductor.
This is your station, lady,
he snapped, and on the downbeat
she stepped to the vita nuova.

A crowd had come to meet her
and they were fond in greeting:

husband, child, and father,
mother, and all the neighbors.

They travel as fast as I do,
she thought, and turned to climb
back to freedom's flying.
The door was shut. The train
streamed off like spilled water.

She faced the crowd and cried:
I love you all but one:
the one who wears my face.
She is the one I fled from.

They said: You took her with you
and brought her back again.
You look sick. Welcome home.

1952

Walled City

I'm going to re-draw myself
with hard clear outlines
cold as asphalt, shinier than tin.
I shall be the envy of the pangolin.
The rolled-up porpentine is not better fortified,
the armadillo will be jealous of my skin.
Come unto me, little children, as far as the fence,
but *Noli Me Tangere* within.

1958

In a Green Shade

We, the god-imagining mammal,
whose flesh is baked of corn or clay:
a sacrificial meal for the compost-goddess—
what nourishment shall we supply
to feed the vigor of our thinking seed?

Will our children bless our bones that tick
in the contaminated earth, or curse
their crazed heirloom, the fallout from our hands?

How can the young take heart from history—
clinical record of their family sickness?
In our disease they dread their raving death
and long debility. They learn that they might be
Attila, Caesar, Hitler, Jenghiz Khan,
bloody uniters of the savage world.

Yet at two trees death gives them measure
of human stature: death at the legal tree
of Rouen, where a country virgin
is winnowed into ash and immortal virtue;

death at the legal tree on the hill of the skull
where a delinquent Jew is nailed to godhead;

but at one tree, at Gaya, in Bihar,
the contemplated navel of the world,
blood is illicit, cruelty renounced.
The living fig tree of the Buddha, fat with seed,
sucks mercy from the breasts of death
and tents our seed against immoderate suns.

Late March–early April, 1959

We Who Are Civilized Salute Ourselves

Strangers in the mob of our resemblances
we posture for one another, greedy
for bravos and the rainy noise of handclaps

set up the cross on hill or lawn
blaspheme each other's holies, cauterize
the foreigner in the flesh and cramp the unassenting mind

Unlike the brutal infant who hams
for his concentric self and roars at his own
pratfalls, we are involved with audiences and enemies

The baby is a little milky beast
battering the five-barred playpen of the senses
while we suck one another's thumb and are not self regardant.

1958 (?)

And Goe the Fooles Among

Fool's Song, King Lear

When death has chastened me
into my final modesty my silence
will be attributed to inability
and not to reticence.

So—while my tongue has power to move—
let me a trifle boldly speak my mind
that my dead silence may reverberate
some truth when I am mute and blind.

Yet even a little truth is far too much
for crooked ears to catch, curled brains to carry.
Truth-tellers must take one of two rewards:
laughter or bloody thorns—both mockery.

Yet mockery may serve. The mockers,
hearing their laughter gone too high and thin,
may grow abashed. And that is a beginning.
Why not be mocked if something may begin?

This was the headlong choice of Fools
even before Jesus. One dare not claim to be
so great a Fool as he. But one can try
using his crazy magnanimity.

1958 (?)

Change

I stand on Caesar's face
(the boss on coin)
and do a swandive
into the notworld

Free fall through space
sweet rocketing between earths.
When you find truth
it is no matter at all

but spirit. When thirty silver
faces of Caesar can learn
to laugh at themselves
even Judas shall wear wings

1948 (?)–1959

The Unreleased

I leave the melting waxworks of my sleep
and come alive to reason. Explicit light
defines my fortune: my inherited self
and all the teaching world.

In libertine sleep I had a dream of fission.
I, the whispering core of an atom,
had thought myself the roaring sky.

To be the center to everything is each man's sentence.
Self is the lodged and little hub enclosed
by an infinite rim that wedges the bars home.

Early 1957 (?)

Monstrous Issue

What shall I do with this anger
which lives in me like a child
and kicks to be born?

What ovary can re-call the embryo?
Neither can I unconceive this anger
this saving grief that craves exit

to sweep the world, destroying fools

1957 (?)

Two Prepositional Endings

Division of Multiplication and Distraction

The sociologists grow grey
imagining what we shall do
when we, the people of the earth,
have more and more been added to

while other gentry bend their skills
to making bomb on bomb on bomb
until it seems far likelier
that we shall be subtracted from.

1958 (?)

Don't Tread on Us

Black shadow
on the dirty pavement
black shadow
of a white man
huge black shadow
of a dwarf white man
with a dirty tongue
saying a dirty word

Black shadow
across a white house
black shadow
cast by an angry sun
black shadow
among forty-nine stars
and the white is streaked
with blood and fire

Wavering flag
of our union.
A new star shines
and other stars go out.
Black shadow
of the ignorant mind
lying over
the minds of children

January, 1959

Let Them Ask Their Husbands

*"And if they will learn anything let
them ask their husbands at home:
for it is a shame for women to speak
in the church."*—I Corinthians 14:35

In human need
of the familiar
I see God
woman-shaped

for God created
woman in Her own image
and I have
my Pauline pride.

1957

Anti-Poem

The valves of silence clap
as jets crash through
and stop the mind.

Fright dries our blood and ink.
The winged horse drowns in the rage
of metal over Helicon.

Heroes in laced and padded mail—
orbital fledglings—try their wings
for a long drop from the nest.

Scorners of the prostrate map—
what can they make of my metric feet
my strophes at the chthonic barrier?

Huge projections of fiction's magic lantern—
lucky for them they've had no time to read
Icarus, Lucifer, and the Tower of Tongues

lay no guilt upon their memories.
No god has told them not to do
what they do not doubt they can.

March, 1959

II. Translations

For to Catch a Whale

(From the French of Jacques Prévert)

Come along and catch a whale, come along and catch a whale,
cried Father in a cranky tone
to Prosper sprawling under the clothespress,
Won't you come and catch a whale, won't you come and catch
    a whale?
What? You don't want to go?
Perhaps you'll tell me why?
Oh why on earth should I go and catch a beast
that never hurt me in the least, Papa?
Go fish it by yourself
if fishing's what you wish.
Poor Mother, I prefer to stay at home with her
and Cousin Gaston.
So Father, rather lonely, in his whaleboat sailed away
over the raging foam. . . .
See the father on the sea
See the son who stays at home
See the whale (who's feeling mean)
And see—oh see Gaston knock over the tureen
Knock over the soup tureen.
The sea was wild
The soup was good
and there sits Prosper in his chair despairing.
Come along and catch a whale! I didn't want to go,
though I don't quite know why.
Perhaps, had I been able to obtain one
I might have tasted it at table,
but see the door burst open wide, and streaming wet,
Father stands and pants and clutches by the tail

the whale which lies across his back.
He casts the beast upon the table, a beautiful blue-eyed whale,
the kind so seldom seen,
and says in a most pathetic tone:
Get busy quickly—carve it, serve it,
I'm starving and I'm thirsty too.
But Prosper springs up from his chair
and stares Papa in the whites of his eyes
blue as the eyes of the whale are blue:
I don't see why I should butcher a creature which never did me harm.
There! You may have my share!
And he throws the knife to the floor.
But the whale is quick to pick it up and flings herself at once on Pop
and stabs him through and through.
Ah ha! says Cousin Gaston,
This makes me think of a butterfly chase,
And now
there's Prosper preparing the bids to the wake
and Mother for her poor man's sake is mourning.
The whale, tears trembling at eyelid, looks at the ruined home
and bursts forth in a cry:
Why—oh why did I kill this pathetic idiot?
Now the others will chase me in put-put boats
and then they'll murder all my tiny tots.
Bursting into disquieting laughter
she swam to the door and sang
to the widow in passing:
Madame, if anyone should ask for me
be so good as to say
The whale's away today
but kindly sit
and wait a bit
She may be back in fifteen years or so. . . .

Spring and fall, 1952

Waste of Time

(From the French of Jacques Prévert)

The millhand stops short
at the factory gate
the fine weather has tugged at his sleeve
and as he turns
and sees the sun
all red round
and smiling in its sizzling sky
he gives a broad
wink
Hey Sun old pal
wouldn't you say
it's kinda dopey
to give a day like this
to a boss?

Early 1950's (?)

Weddings and Banquets

(From the French of Jacques Prévert)

In the ruins of a cathedral
a butcher cries like a calf over the death of a bird
and lying on the crazed flagstones
a bell overthrown and cracked
exposes its rusty clapper
reminding one of a large obscene priest
with wind-lifted cassock
and in the crumbled sacristy
three or four rascals in caps
take the collection
on the occasion of the marriage of Heaven and Hell
All this is going on in England
partly in honor of the French Revolution
as well as the death of Lewis XVI
The bridegroom is known as William Blake
He is quite naked and altogether correct
but he keeps his hat on his head
to guard the Holy Ghost within
which is the spirit of contradiction
When anyone asks—Spirit are you there
that dove invariably replies with an engaging smile
No
When the wedding is over William Blake will make a present of it
    to the butcher
who will forget his dead parakeet
and go back to killing cattle
with a big mallet
We are not to be compared with a bird
thinks William Blake
with his mind on something else
which is neither more nor less than the spectacle
of a dazzling girl invited by someone or other to the wedding

and who is really lovely and just as naked as he is
A beauty
thinks William Blake a beauty of a radiant calm
pure as red wine
and innocent as Spring
And he gazes at her because he desires her
and she gazes at him because she desires him
when there appears a big Barbary duck
playing a tune of all times and places on his barrel organ
and the wedding begins
the wedding proper
as William Blake precisely states
because there are some things so clumsily
and so badly said
Is it for the Mass that you say that
asks an old man with the head of a prophet or bishop
and a most argumentative air
But William Blake is a gentleman
a nice man as they say in England
and has no wish to discuss with a bishop
the wedding day of Heaven and Hell
and who in any case suspects
that this is also the day of his own wedding
seeing that the girl is so enchanting
and that he loves her beyond all doubt
and that she probably loves him too
He is therefore quite content to say
to the man with the head of a bishop or a prophet or a safety pin

> "As the caterpillar chooses the fairest leaves to lay her eggs on,
> so the priest lays his curse on the fairest joys."

Well then on with the music
We'll speak of the Mass some other time
And since he has said On with the music
the music goes on
and behind it the dazzling girl
who smiles at William Blake

because he once said

"Prisons are built with stones of law, Brothels with bricks of
    religion."

And she gives him her arm
and everything else along with it
and who is happy now
but William
William Blake

1959 (?)

Song of the Bird Catcher
(From the French of Jacques Prévert)

Bird that has so sweet a flight
Bird so red and warm as blood
Bird so tender mocking bird
Bird that suddenly is stirred
Bird that beats about the wood
Bird that longs to fly away
Bird bewildered lonely bird
 that wants to live
 that wants to sing
 that wants to cry
Bird so red and warm as blood
Bird that has so sweet a flight
It is your heart my charming child
That beats its wing all sad and wild
Against your breast so firm so white.

January, 1958

The Dazzled Ones

(From the French of Jean-Arthur Rimbaud: September, 1870)

Smudged in the murk and in the snow,
Against the ventilator's glow,
   Their butts rounded,

Five tattered tykes upon their knees
Watch the baker mix and squeeze
   The thick blond bread.

They see the strong white arms that roll
The dough, and in a luminous hole
   Lay it with care.

They wait the good bread's making while
The baker with his buttered smile
   Croons an old air.

They crouch there, quiet and intent,
As if they found that radiant vent
   Warm as a breast.

When, fashioned for some midnight spread,
The brioche rolls of twisted bread
   Come forth at last,

And under the smoke-blackened beams
The crickets chirp and the bread gleams,
   The ravished rogues

At whom life rises from a stove
Pulse with a sense of sudden love
   Under their rags.

They feel themselves in life's good hold,
These shivering Christkids gnawed by cold,
    And cluster near,

Pushing pink muzzles to the grille,
Chattering, as they gaze their fill
    Through Heaven's door.

Poor puppies—there they pray and press
Against that gate to happiness,
    Their small knees skinned,

Their breeches bursting at the seam,
Their thin shirts shuddering in the stream
    of the winter wind.

March, 1952

The Compassionate Torturers
(From the French of Victor Hugo)

Torture chambers are not pleasure domes.
No-one lives more than five hours in such rooms.
Young men who go in come out grown old.
The judge, the artist-torturer, impelled
one by the code, the other by his craft,
devote themselves to work upon the soft
medium of human flesh, conspire to join
red iron and Roman law, and spare no pain
to win the avowal needed. At their touch
hair, muscle, nail, and bone feel horror's twitch.

Loudness of screams is governed by which fiber
shudders, which nerve responds to that skilled labor.
A man becomes a harpsicord whereon
the bloody fingers of the player run
the scales of agony. Do not be sure
the hearts of torturers hold nothing more
than menace, for this duty makes them grieve.
They sweeten torture with a touch of love.

Resistance saddens them, and as they broach
body, to come at mind, their tongues beseech.
They are paternal as they supplicate,
stooping above the sufferer, regret
the need to blind an eye to make the mouth
vomit, in its extremity, an oath.

There have been torturers of a grain so fine
they've quoted poems to assuage the pain
and coax the secret that the captive kept.
And others, big with empathy, have wept.

1959 (?)

Art Poétique
(From the French of Paul Verlaine)

Above all—music, and in that
choose the dynamic—the unforeseen—
but keep it vague and soluble in air,
containing nothing that weighs down and fixes.

Be careful, too, never to choose your words
without a sort of knowing carelessness.
What is better than the grey song
where the precise and imprecise are joined?

Consider eyes shining behind veils,
the mighty day trembling at the point of noon,
the autumn sky touched with warmth,
a litter of vivid stars in the blue.

What is needed always is nuance—
not color—nothing but suggestion.
It is only nuance that betroths
the dream to the dream, the flute to the horn.

Shun most of all the epigram,
the cruel spirit and unholy laughter,
which make the inward eye to weep—
and shun the garlic of low cookery.

Take eloquence and twist its neck.
And while you are at it, you'll do well
to make your rhyme a little reasonable.
If you don't watch it, who knows where it will go?

What shall I say of the honors of rhyme?
What deaf infant or benighted idiot
has forged for us this penny trinket
which rings false and hollow under the file?

Music first and music always!
Oh let your verse be an affair of wings
so that one feels it to be a soul in flight
to other skies and other loves.

Let your verse be a bold hazard—
a scattering in the crinkled morning wind
that carries with it odors of mint and thyme . . .
And all the rest is literature.

1959 (?)

Another
England

1941

For My Mother and My Father

I

Another England

Remember: the willowed lawn, the wall of laurel,
the hybrid roses, the terrace thick with thyme.
There we walked in a wished world veined already
with rivering cracks. But love was our concern.
Darwin was our philosopher. We knew
survival of the British to be a cosmic fiat.
Noblesse oblige we learned, but did not learn
history well enough to foretell disaster,
and could not read in the farmer's averted face
the anger and hatred of men grown sick of tenantry.

Remember: the busy dance-floor—matrimonial market
where obedient bargains for the sake of breed
were struck to music. We were young then, and a battleship
was an arsenal of adventure and love. Wine at dinner
and a seated toast to the king, and the boatswain's mate
piping punctiliously to the bored sea lord
the shrill salute of custom.

We had not been told that the sailor was syphilitic
and society worse diseased. We did not know
how many sleepless peoples of our empire
prayed to their first gods for the sun to set.
(God save the Queen and God forgive all kings.)
Our problems were so urgent: how to find
the right modiste; three plumes from the denuded ostrich
to nod at a royal drawing-room; the fees for Dartmouth;
income enough for gold braid and champagne.

I hated war and loved your epaulettes.
Yet I was not indifferent to the praises

of bored young men who loathed your uniform.
Applause for Dali of the school of Freud!
R.S.V.P. to the Duchess—bring your golf clubs
and get on the right side of God over the week-end.
(War is as déclassé as ectoplasm
and Kipling staler than a hand grenade.)

Hello, Piccadilly!
We're safe for a thousand years.
The devil's chopping wood at Doorn,
so Leicester Square—three cheers!

They dance a war dance in Berlin,
in Rome a tarantella,
while here we go gathering nuts in May
around a broad umbrella.

It's a long, long way to Tipperary,
a longer way to peace,
but a short, blind rush from the Battle of the Marne
to Munich, Dunkirk, Greece.

Remember: May Week at Cambridge with the great marquees
profaning the precincts; sex under the rose;
the sweet sliding hours on the Cam; intrusion of girls
on adolescent nerves of aging dons.
Remember the pelting of the pony hooves
at Ranelagh and Roehampton when the mallets whirled.
(The British conquered India to learn her games.)

Remember: tea and thin bread-and-butter carried in
to chintz-chaired drawing-rooms by decorous maids;
tennis on the lawn—three balls held up for service
in the one hand, like a pawnbroker's sign,
tossed to the moody weather and racqueted
rather with exuberance than competitive ardor:
Your game—well played!—Remember the leaning sails—
yachts flung like peregrine falcons from the wind's wrist
among the blunt and tedious fishing boats.

Remember Sunday village peace: accustomed worship
in little churches of stone that were the fossiled flowers
of faith more active in a time not so safe.
God, who had been a refuge, had become
a golden-edged security. He stifled a yawn
at the good works of the rector's wife and looked
vainly for a prophet or a proud rebellion.

The banners of knights remember, standing tall
in the Chapel of St. George at Windsor Castle—
standing like harboured sails in the windless air
and cloying dusk of chivalry. Remember how
in Westminster Abbey the hierarchy of Christendom
walked with a lulling majesty; how the choir
built up its composite voice to a sky of stone
till the groined vaults cast back that tonal image
to the dark waters of the waiting senses.

Remember Maundy Thursday when the king
humbly in the high Abbey amongst his lords
gave ritual money to the chosen poor
so that they might remember the king's bounty
and Christ's sweet pity, and hush their mutinous hearts.

Terror is quick. Wounds go deep
in street or flesh where bombs fall thick.
The mind grows sick when wounds are slow.

Where poverty's black bomb has burst,
the stricken houses, roof and wall,
shudder on the air and go
into a long and soundless fall.

Home was the loved word then, and not alone
where homes were lovable, but in the rotted hut
and sick-jointed human stable; to the hopeless woman
broken by ten births, and the caught spirits of her children—

ten wretched atonements for rapture or ignorance.
The miner, digger of coal and dividends
for warmth and ease of other than his kindred,
yawned, scrubbed his grimy body at a pump,
wondered mutely at his dusty life
and cried, on the right occasions: *The King, God Bless Him!*
Patriots of the playing fields of Eton
brag of victorious Waterloos. Let it pass.
There indeed the thoroughbred, flanneled legs
learn the long stride of leaders. But do you forget
the Saturday-washed legs of Billingsgate
and the Midlands' factory feet that follow with pain and patience
and are buried or lost for loyalty?

We forgot them then. We did not know them then,
nor the black-nailed fingers and the eyes quenched by work,
nor the tempered Saxon hearts still cast in the mold of Alfred.

You too, my dear, were Saxon, ruddy and fair,
with an island heart, true and not soon invaded,
but the speech of your lips and your way of thinking tainted
and sweetened with a Norman elegance:
I loved you as I loved England. When we paused
one evening under a tree on the hilltop and looked down
to the eternal valleyed village of man's hope,
and said: *This is our country, this is our peaceful home,*
we did not know how the very love of it
had half betrayed it to an envious evil,
nor how our carelessness of what we loved
had sown futility to reap revolt.

The long, good future promised in our kiss
changed with the world—changed soon. The tranquil love,
guarded and fruitful, of an English wife,
was not my destiny, nor England's, either.
For me another continent, another lover
and another happiness. For you—another England.
For you and for all men another world.

When I went down to Plymouth dock
my watch was slow three hundred years.
The ship had sailed. But neither clock
nor sailing schedule keeps the mind
from setting forth to seek its peers,
from taking ship at last to find
the westland of its wish for growth.
Three centuries I sailed behind
the free forefathers of my thought,
but in the land of freedom's oath,
where I had looked for all I prize,
I found less faith than I had brought.
I found that time had warped a chain
of custom and of compromise
about the body, heart and brain.
Then, had I taken ship in vain?
Or might I, tardy to arrive,
help fan the pilgrim fire alive?

Yesterday's crisis is tomorrow's chrysalis.
The nations rise and subside in a rhythm of courage and shame.
There is no innocent country. There are a few
which, culpable, have yet redeemed themselves
and roused a yawning greatness out of sleep.
Others, cracking upon the inward chaos
of a contracting morality, reeled and collapsed;
and the mightiest of these is France, sister of freedom.
Rather for revolution than for war
the angry living embers of the people of France
have kindled above the stature of their kings
and made a beacon of man's basic grandeur.
But war as well has been an answered challenge.
The fire of nineteen-fourteen roared to a smoky apex,
waned to a faint conclusion, dwindled to a single tongue
speaking to tomorrow from an arch of doubtful triumph—
a nameless tongue rehearsing a half-learned truth
to a world not tutored yet in the majesty of selfless man.
The sleeper wakes. We thought he slept so well,

but, quick with grief, he has a thing to tell
has hatched his dream-tormented ghost from the tomb's black shell.

The ghost was crazed by the bloody clay on the eyes.
Half blind with death it still perceives the lies
that men call peace on earth. The disgusted bones must rise.

The world's guilt walks. The living, with rising hair,
with arms oblique, salute what comes to share
its own insomnia with their own despair.

France of the high humanities flowering out of Chartres
and lifting the wave of Abélard and Villon
from abundant intellect and starving gutter to topple the Bastille;
France, divided and frightened behind her imaginary line,
has been sold down the Rhine by her leaders. Let them eat pretzels.
And let the invader swarm. The buildings, arrested flux
of industry and time, are still intact
and make good monuments. Only the spirit is harmed.

Only the spirit. But England made another choice.
Only the body is harmed. The spirit blazes
above the rubbled beauty of her towns,
above the reckoning of her ancient sins,
above the shambled children and crazed mothers
and the men weary and grim and exalted by sacrifice.

My dear, where are you now?—what bearing or performing?
Are you accoutered with metal and with fire
to be the dragon and St. George combined
against the advancing Robot? Or do you lie quenched
and scattered, sinew from sinew, cancelled out
from struggle or hope by a bomb in Coventry?

Nucleus of time and timelessness, we turn
on the axis of helpless change.
War and death on the far circumference of our thought,
creeping spores of death on the curved boundary,

on the turning sphere.
Calamity amongst the seeds of the stars,
in the strewn shells on shore,
in dune-grass and beached withering jellyfish.
Calamity in the white arc of the swooping gull,
terror in the scaled silver body leaping,
terror in the pale crab hiding in the whelk's forlorn house,
and terror in me, personal terror, blind and whimpering,
horror of the threat to established littleness and strength,
of termites channeling the deep foundations.

None can ignore the long march of the tide up the shore,
nor the long march of led men, of selves relinquished to a leader,
against our amorphous system, our life without fusion of purpose.
They come forward, encroaching, mindless as the sea.
They break over us, shining, crying *Heil!* and *Viva!*
And we stand quiet with mazed minds, sucking the candies of our
        nursery peace,
while boundaries go down and dykes are broken
and the flood comes licking at our neat white porches.

The bombs break more than buildings, or lives, or dreams.
They break the pattern of a past we had no courage
to cash for a new venture. Let them fall.
We shall not now return to the laurels and dancing.
There is no path through space, there is no path through time
to lead us there again. I in another continent
and you in another age have lost that moment.
The house is a ghost. The terrace is roof for a shelter.
The horses are requisitioned. The lawns are ploughed.
Near the bombed house the servants stand bewildered.
In the deep mines the miners crouch to a hazard
closer than bombs. They feel their black roof shake,
their tunnels shrink toward the fiery day
when they may straighten to their full man's height.
The factories spin, and every bullet struck
is a man's or a woman's pledge to speed the hour

of final waking and late recompense.
They will not know at first what they must do,
but their eyes are England's, and not averted from danger,
and hold in their frightened pupils the small gold seed
of freedom that shall break the feudal husk.

March to May, 1941

Cross of Steel

How many ages of ordeal by wind and light
tempered the hawk's mail and prepared his eye for the sun?

The hawk-men stand at their parapets and sweep
all other frontiers with eyes of scrutiny.
Their heads turn—so do vultures'—they swivel in unison
as heads of spectators at a tennis match.

The hawks of Italy, the hawks of Germany, the hawks of Russia
flock, mailed and medalled, each about a leader.
They crowd in close to the magnetic presence
that integrates their mass and cancels their separate futilities.
At the wing-lift of the leader, at its identical tilt,
the wings of the lieutenants move in absolute sympathy,
for the will of the individual is abrogated
in favor of mass impulse and mass objective.

Under the hawk-men the crab-men, the new crustaceans,
colonies of men around whom fear has grown
its monstrous carapace of tank and submarine.
The individual is man no longer, but the machine
whose soul, whose life is the sum of many men.
For flesh and blood, that once were holy enough for sacrament,
are now become fuel, protein for monsters of metal,
and the cry of a man or a child broken by violence
is no more than the cellular revulsion of a chopped cabbage.

In what pride we have lived for many generations!
We have claimed to be the perfection of fish, beast, bird.
Are we weary now of our long supremacy
that we turn without protest to the policies of the lesser kingdoms?
Great fish in murderous shoals gang the tidal depths
and we are of their company. Great birds
wheel in the sky for lambs and carrion

and we have joined them. Terrible armoured beasts
once thundered through the forests of great ferns,
and we begin to ape them on an earth where soon no tree will care
    to grow.

Farewell to man unless he be redeemed
by such a vision of himself as Christ once was
before man's cunning made a cross of steel
more terrible even than the cross of wood,
and nailed his godhead not in the sun's light
but in the interior darkness, the bloody iron maiden,
the cruciform casket of terrible enclosing metal,
so insulated that the cry of God
cannot be heard—even to grant forgiveness.

Early 1941 (?)

Cock Crow

The cocks that cry from town to town
assail Time's gate and break it down.

Through centuries, by links of sound,
to Christ's dark night this night is bound.

The same proud bugling pierced the sky
when Peter did his Lord deny.

The red dawn flows across my sill.
I dare not look upon the hill

lest I should see the deed new-done:
three crosses black against the sun.

Early 1940 (?)

As It Was in the Beginning

We have been taught how in the French retreat
from Moscow, vileness occurred, and the world continued;
how Christians were served for lions' preposterous meat;
how God was crucified; how slaves, strong-sinewed,
were agony harnessed to move a magnificent fleet.
Yet in those sorrowful times the artist and peasant
strove with eyes inward or earthward, experienced sweet
and terrible deeps of joy in their terrible present.

Cry against your day as men have forever done,
believing it the worst—believing themselves to inherit
the age of darkness after the age of the sun.
I say all days are evil, since first the spirit
moved on the waters. The bomb, the gun
were patterned in chaos; so, indeed, were the breasts of desire
and the beauty of beasts that, born to terror, run
like music around creation's wheel of fire.

1940 (?)

For the Public Good

A woman runs shrieking
through the streets of space
a lost child seeking.

Have you seen a little lad,
gold hair, bright face,
in clean white clad?

Home she comes hurrying,
calmed of her terror,
a thin child carrying.

But Madam—you've seized
that waif by an error.
He is ragged—diseased!

O fools that impede me!
All are the same.
All hapless things need me.

They seize her, they bind her,
they publish her name.
She is mad. Never mind her.

1940 (?)

Thinking of Finland, 54 Degrees below Zero

Can you forget them?—I, my friend,
am plagued by them. They haunt my table:
the starved, the broken and the blind.

We know now: there is nothing noble
in being shattered by a bomb
to help one's country in its trouble.

But I should never care to claim
that I am nobler than the fighter,
being well-fed and warm at home.

Perhaps, indeed, I might do better
to play his stakes of death and life
than be so haunted
                and so safe.

January, 1940 (?)

Afternoon Tea

To MARGRIT ROSENSTOCK-HUESSY

The dusky Chinese tea, tasting of shadow,
hot from the thin cups, comforts our dry throats.
Our thoughts are all of war. We speak our thoughts.
The window opens on the sunlit meadow.

The rusks are sweet. Our taste of them is bitter.
Our tongues are heavy with a lost world's grief
as still we practise, for a short while safe,
a lost world's rite of tea and toast and butter.

A German woman and an English woman
and a young Jewess in a neutral land—
freed of our flags, we strive to comprehend
the rupture of a world we love in common.

The decorous room with sanity encloses
our bodies, but our outraged thoughts are fled
to cities where our sisters, screaming mad,
hunt for small corpses in the wreck of houses.

Fall, 1939

Nunc Dimittis

When womb-walled hangs my child
  in man's own image
I shall not forget how he is nailed
  already on the cross of his own damage,
already destined to death
  and before death, grief,
already the hero and the victim, both,
  of enigmatic life.

Shall I anticipate with joy
  his leaving the womb?
Would I not rather let him stay
  in that safe home?
Would I not rather bid him back
  to chaos, unconceived,
than urge him forth to terror and the wreck
  of God by man enslaved?

Sleep in the shapeless dark!
  Child! Come not forth!
Man wreaks too hideous a work
  in this, the little country of the earth.
I, who am woman, betrayed
  by man's great sin,
swear I shall not contribute to the deed
  by bringing forth a son.

O silence! Be complete!
  Stars, be extinguished!
Now the world ends. Now Bach is mute,
  Prometheus no more anguished.
Euclid, goodnight! Sleep well with the dead planets!
  Forget the wasted chronicle of time,

my Shakspere! In this end of aeons and minutes
evoke no more the dream.

Summon no more the courage
    and the terror
of man who makes his bitter marriage
    with death and horror.
But, lest I falter in my wish for sleep,
    torment me with no memory of love.
Do not deceive my sorrow with the hope
    that it is sweet to live,

sweet to behold the day,
    a privilege to share
sorrow and hunger with men beneath the sky,
    or any pain or fear.

So long as love hides somewhere on the earth,
    so long as the eyes see, and the stars burn,
then let my child grow valiant and come forth!
    His mother is forsworn.

January, 1940

I Crucified My Brother

I crucified my brother
on a cross of wood.
The nailed grain understood.
The tree could feel his grief.
The tree put forth a leaf,
flower and leaf and root,
and bore compassionate fruit.

I crucified my brother
on a cross of steel.
The metal could not feel.
Flower nor leaf nor root
foretold the pitiless fruit
that ripened and rained down
onto the open town.

Early 1941

Path of Fire

Stark in the settling dust
they lie who late were men.
Water nor wine nor crust
will they desire again.

Quiet lies the town
where hell has hurried by,
with fury mowing down
those who were there to die.

With garments wet and red,
torn flesh and splintered bone,
they sleep on ruin's bed,
heavier than stone.

Look on the carnage. Gaze
till you be reconciled:
remember all your days
the remnant of a child.

1940 (?)

Newsreel

Keep to your seat. Be chary of belief.
It's only a movie, for the most part faked.
These are paid actors simulating grief,
trundling prop chattels. Where the guns have raked
buildings, apparently—where bombs make rubble,
it's only the sort of thing that Hollywood can do without much trouble.

Not even on an island of devils would men be treated
like this—you fool—no matter what their sins.
It's only a movie. For God's sake—keep seated.
It won't be long before the screen begins
to show the loves of Hedy, or, with luck,
the bright brutalities of Donald Duck.

Early 1941

Kwannon

Kwannon is a borrowed goddess:
Chinese mercy in Japan.
She suckles in her silken bodice
a little murdered man.

1940 (?)

II

The Maker

It is the fashion to speak in the falling cadence
of disillusion. The world ends with a whimper,
not with a bang, and it is merely prudence
thus to foretell and so to feel the temper
of now and tomorrow, the poet being only the doctor
to take the pulse and diagnose the ailment,
always considering death the one known factor.
I hate that falsehood. I hate the time's defilement
of art by politics. It is the gift of the poet
to contradict chaos, to hear the YES! of the womb
and loud along the ear of man to say it,
making another space, and a new time.

1939 (?)

For the Lonely One

I weep for the lonely one, the one passed over,
who dreams of love and weeps upon her bed,
who dreams of love and never has known a lover,
who has not had the sweetness I have had.

I grieve for her who for herself lies grieving,
and long to cry to her—Go forth, go forth
and look for love that is so well worth having,
the lack of which can darken heaven and earth.

She lies upon her virgin's bed of torture
and dreams of love both sweeter and less sweet
than love can be that has its proper nurture,
and all her dreams of love shall turn to hate:

hate of herself and her inordinate hunger,
hate of the world too blind to see her need,
and hate of luckier ones, and all her anger
breaks in a wave of sorrow on my bed.

1940 (?)

Vita Nuova

Christians, after thirteen hundred,
blenched at the plague, beheld black death
break their loves and fell their kindred.
Cadaver dread annealed their faith,
sealed to God their frantic oath.
Kneeling to the doom that smote them
they reared a bulwark of the myth
of Christian heaven to requite them.

Old gods are folded in their triptychs.
Death dwindles. Now the latter saints
rout devils with their antiseptics;
sin is absolved at needles' points;
clairvoyance of the lens presents
the priests of space with revelation
of miracle. The mind surmounts
terror, and finds a new devotion.

1940 (?)

Locked in Amber

Substantial color walls the mind around,
yet, though it sees through amber,
never dream
that it is dead within its yellow chamber.

Observe the strictured insect in its mold
of petrified pale resin
whereof the gleam
should make a splendor of the straitest prison.

The latticed eyes look out, not wholly drowned:
the wings—crazed, futile hammers,
strain to shatter
the gelid sunlight of ten million summers.

Break—O my mind!—this curse of glassy gold.
Clean from the clasping color
of dream and matter
rise free to daylight with a wingéd valor.

1937 (?)

De Profundis

I

There are things the blood remembers
for knowing which the brain is still too young.
The blood speaks in the arterial chambers
of circumstance forgotten and shapes that sprang
from chaos and subsided into jungle
long before man was mammal. We can place
no seal upon them, and the mind can angle
deep for an answer and not hook a guess.

II

Ocean and planet, iron and hair and blood
spring not more certain out of matter's womb
than speech or music or the myth of god
reared from the chasm of the racial dream.
The measured form, the artificial pattern
of fugue and sonnet from the dark flow forth
even as the feathers of the speckled bittern,
even as the fern upfronding from the earth.

1939 (?)

The Eternal

Man imperishably stands
through his thousand destinies.
There are planets in his eyes,
there are aeons in his hands.

Time in him is ever now:
yesterday is in his veins
and tomorrow in his loins
and forever on his brow.

1939 (?)

Sky

Better than Brunelleschi
I can construct a dome:
the mind can warp space
to fit the eye's false frame.

Of edgeless emptiness
I vault me a blue prison,
its arc the meridian,
its lip the seen horizon.

Pantheon of my thought,
roof of the sight's illusion,
home for the frightened spirit
raised of the stones of vision.

For truth is beyond form,
but man, whose soul is simple,
must house the ineffable god
in the apparent temple.

1940 (?)

Coral and Chlorophyll

Chemical or Euclidean, the crystal
shapes in the falling flake, or in the mind.
This is creation's chastity—the Vestal
structure of beauty formally defined.

Fever of chlorophyll—the proud and floral
color of blood, hold Aphrodite's grief,
hushed only in the skeleton and the coral
and in the golden drying of the leaf.

Early 1940 (?)

We

The year goes under.
I see the wind tear
the tree's gold hair.
I see it render
that which is earth's
to earth: the ash
of the fire of the Fall.
I feel the North's
funereal
thin breath of ice
burn my flesh,
blow once, blow twice
on me,
on the tree.

We share that breath,
our limbs hang low,
heavy with snow,
heavy with death.

1940 (?)

Kwan Yin

The slanted eyes
the two hands like one flower
the raiment musical about the limbs
peace, like a quiet shower
of brief rain
bringing the noon of pain
its cool relief.

The tapers bud with fire.
The long slow hymns
rise from the carven choir,
lifting above the world
the sorrow of things human.
Hail Mary, full of grace!
Blessed art thou among women.

The white hands curled
around the heart of flame
the mantle folded like a fugue of peace
the sweet and bitter name
the pitiful eyes
the crown of Paradise
the mouth of grief.

1938 (?)

Gloria Mundi

The contrivers of beauty
fix and send forth the transient hour
beyond its epoch.

Silver, marble,
ivory, glass and clay,
the antique shapes
hammer upon the present.

The bells, the gongs,
the little lotus feet
of the court of Ch'ien Lung
are silent, are still.

A core of dust is Pharaoh
in the golden windings
that deceive not death,

and Caesar is dust
and Timour is lame no more
and the arrow wound is healed
in Harold's eye.

For the page is turned
the fans are folded
and the shields are hung.

But on our walls
hang silks of imperial yellow
embroidered with five-toed
fabulous blue dragons
and the soldiers of William
are stitched in eternal conquest

by Matilda's maidens
in the dark towers of Bayeux.

The Tanagran Eros
the Mycenaean sword
the enameled ikon
and the lapis bowl
are tangible to us

and touching them
we touch the dead.

Not alone flesh but silk
fades in the long day.
Granite even as bone
is fluid in eternity.

Nevertheless
we lean upon our looms
to anchor our ghosts.

We cast the wind in bronze.

Early 1939–early 1941

Fox of Fire

Flee their folly, shimmering fox,
till they run you lame.
Blast the lichens, brand the rocks
with your feet of flame.

Flee upon your futile rounds—
nowhere shall you hide.
Over brook and bracken, hounds
pour their crying tide.

Scornful is the smiling sneer
fixed upon the mask,
covering the heart whose fear
may no mercy ask.

Grass of gold and blazing leaf
shall not shield your fire.
Thieving men who call you thief
hunt you till you tire.

Haunt the thicket, glimmering ghost,
where your blood is spilled.
Man it is whose cause is lost
when the fox is killed.

1939 (?)

Married

As the wave carves cliffs to water's curve
and cove and sea have shape reciprocal,
my spirit has been brought at last to the world's look.

I lacked this imprint in my primitive springtime.
I came a stranger, violent of will, and virgin,
jealous for truth and desirous of revolution.

Now my volition tends to far other ends.
The strange child has become in life's strange house
a spouse, submissive to paradox, big with enigma.

1940 (?)

III

Acknowledgment

Thank you for silence,
for saying nothing at all
when the moment was too big,
the heart too small.

Early February, 1940

Extrovert

When Julia glances at her watch
her wrist turns on its rhythmic bones
as if her pulse should strive to catch
the metronomic monotones.

It is as if in Julia's thoughts
Time's an insect under crystal,
or a target struck with shots
cracking from a pigmy pistol.

She does not know that Time, indeed,
is a dragon eating the sun and moon
in infinite caves of starry dread.
She knows it is late in the afternoon
and time to be dining, soon.

Late 1940

Gamine

Under the virgin moon
whose gaze is cool and cynical,
a cat explores the night
with footsteps sly and finical.

The cat is black as chaos
and silken as deceit
and rhythmic as a Negro song
upon her sensual feet.

By rainpools, over litter,
she walks with perspicacity.
I call. She stops. She stares,
intrigued by such audacity.

I stoop to smooth her sides.
She swoons to me at once,
lifting a rumbling throat
in rapturous response.

Her body shakes with song.
She strikes ecstatic attitudes—
too musical with life
for shyness and its platitudes.

Early 1940

Sculptor

The attitude is one of dream,
the eyes are lowered in devotion
above the head whose tempered gleam
sets waves of copper light in motion.

Archaic curls of chastened fire,
set flat about the balanced skull,
beneath the practised hands acquire
the impress of the beautiful.

Pygmalion, satisfied, serene,
binds in a net the tutored hair,
then, with a movie magazine,
waves Galatea to a chair.

Early 1940

Forager

The muscular squirrel in hyphenated leaps
spans his brisk way. He very wisely keeps
his equilibrium aft. The nervous tail
sees to it that the footing does not fail
aground or treed, and leaves the quick small brain
free for a commissariat campaign.

1940 (?)

Vive le Roi!

The pheasant wakes me in the lucent morning
with his doubled cry.
A conscious weather-cock that, stiffly turning,
declares the breaking day—

he wanders in his splendor in the meadow,
lording his quiet hen,
or royally consorting with his shadow
turfed by the climbing sun.

A pheasant? No—a phoenix flamed with feathers
fronded of light and fire.
He had unnumbered khans for his forefathers;
he is the apparent heir

of treasure and tradition made eternal
in him, the ultimate lord,
the deathless, sleek and delicately carnal
contemptuous bird.

Spring, 1940

Icarus in the White Mountains

With spears of hickory for shoes,
he whips the hill, the silver hone.
He burns the singing snow, he falls
oblique as on a falcon's cruise,
then diagraphs a herringbone
as, slow and wingless, up he crawls.

Early 1939 (?)

IV

The Village

Here are the faces, old and seamed and wise,
or young and grave, of all the towns of time;
the eternal boy who in the schoolyard plays,
teasing a girl eternally the same.

Calcium of the bone and cellulose
of tree and building, stuff of man and dwelling,
form and go forth in flux that does not cease,
in vigor rising full and over-filling

to flow beyond the keeping of the breath,
so that the skeleton, so small in the womb,
spills in the end to shadow, sleeps beneath
the gravestones where the morbid weepers come;

so that the church and farmhouse, joyfully built
and whitened like a memory of Greece,
grieve in their beams and dwindle, fault by fault,
to ruin and the records of the place.

And the sun rises and the moon goes under,
and Eben dies and little Saul is born;
the church-bells riot in their tower of tinder;
the corn is gathered and the planets turn.

Early 1940

November Abstract

All the green summer through it came incarnate
in scented snowflakes clustered on frail umbels
of Queen Anne's Lace, in goldenrod, in cymbals
of dandelion. My fingers have uptorn it
delicately in orchid, trillium, clover,
hepatica and all the tribe of daisies
and lodged it briefly in my bowls and vases:
beauty to ease my spirit of its fever.

And now I wander through the blond, bleached acres
sucked of their color by the North's sharp hunger,
and with a sober joy, from earth no longer
vital, but brought to death's pale browns and ochres,
I pluck the residual beauty, the bones of glamour:
grey goldenrod, brown burdocks, milkweed purses
and skeletal grass, and their dry beauty pierces
my kindred bones beyond the thrust of summer.

November, 1939

Leaf from a Notebook

Under palmetto fans the rattlesnake
slides sweetly without anger. Tree orchids hang
on stunted pine, on cypress, choosing from air
their delicate provender. Mosquitoes rise
on water-colored wings from fecund water
and dance toward flesh or fruit with slender thirsting spears.
Lizards, coral and bronze, with sun-spark eyes,
kindle the speary grasses. The far cool smash of surf
quenches a little the inland parch of noon.
The Seminole village sleeps, drowsy with singing flies,
drowsy with the death of the race. Caryatids of cloud
stand strong on the flat country, with a look of snow,
bearing a blue entablature. Above the rafts
of river hyacinth, suddenly there are wings:
the sky is circled by a noose of herons.

1938 or early 1939

Five Hokku

I

The mailed fish, balanced
on crystal stairs of water,
swims too in the mind.

II

The old are precious.
Value them as gold, hard-earned
and soon to be spent.

III

Look not to heaven
for fragrance. Look to flowers
whose roots drink darkness.

IV

The birch tree's whiteness
reveals a choir of colors
against the new snow.

V

I have folded my life
like wings. Desire, I said, dies.
I will practise peace.

1940 (?)

Vermonters

These are the people living in this land:
proud and narrow, with their eyes on the hills.
They ask no favors. Their lips defend
with speech close rationed their hoarded souls.

You cannot love them or know them at all
unless you know how a hardwood tree
can pour blond sugar in a pegged-up pail
in the grudging thaw of a February day.

1940 (?)

Cartoon for a Weaver

The unicorn with horn of ivory
slopes his head in amorous slavery
upon the pure lap of a virgin only
who in a tapestry sits young and queenly.

The unicorn moves shyly out of leaves,
poses imperiled on devotional hooves,
collapses to his knees, felled by the shafts
of innocence. The sickly virgin lifts
his muzzle in her tender boneless hands.

Her gaze goes far. Past the cadaverous hounds
that flush sleek pheasants for equestrian lords,
past the stitched flowers and the static birds,
past love and venery her long look goes.

She sees no beauty with her creweled eyes,
but in the lilied valley of her skirt
the silver creature lays his constant heart.

Late 1939

Photo Graph

I saw a frieze of golden cows
go beautiful along a road,
and timelessness was on their brows
as delicate and calm they strode.

The poignant profile, old as thought,
processional through morning light,
against a fadeless film I caught
along the iris lens of sight.

1939 (?)

Song for December

Gladly I saw the windy chute
of Autumn's furious avalanches.
The leafless crab tree, thick with fruit
struck dark by frost on iron branches,

stands like a tree of Chinese art,
an abstract on a silken void.
You may choose Summer. For my part
I quicken to the lean, uncloyed

and celibate Winter. Then the cold
bodies the breath before the eye;
platinum twilights, drained of gold,
lie wide and clean in the freezing sky;

safe in the seed is Spring, packed little;
beech leaves flicker like fire gone low;
and cricket corpses, scattered and brittle,
are ruined fiddles under the snow.

Late 1940

Vermont Evening

White houses inhabit the dusk,
   their windows gold with light
   as combs with honey.

Green the dusk,
   green the space between the elms
   and the sky green

and the sky lilac
   and amethyst and
   apple blossom

and the moon a sunflower
   turning, turning
   its face to the sun.

1939

New England Extract

From Greece the porch,
from Normandy the spire,
Scotland the dogma,
Galilee the fire.
Pine-boarded, Ladies' Guilded,
groved in birch:
the Holy Ghost's
and Isaac Damon's church.

Late 1939

Song for May

I shall go where water is rushing
cold and quick with the shine of Spring.
Taste of water is in the wind.
The pond is sweet with silk of the sky.

Snow has swum to the sea in rivers.
Foam and spume are woven of snow.
Tree-sap clambers on stairs of fiber.
Amber meadows are broken with blades.

Birds wheel north to the ear of waiting.
Blood is green with a catkin rain.
I shall go where water is shallow,
where yellow shoots of the willow show.

1940 (?)

Antiphon

I

Break then and break and break
with deep and bitter ache
the heart of man, O Lord!

And is it then thy will
that man shall give thee still
more than thou wilt afford?

For man, who suffers sorrow without surcease,
still is required to count upon thy mercies.

II

Cry then, O man!—complain,
thou worm brought forth by rain,
thou shadow of my grief!

All that thou art, I wrought,
thy semblance and thy thought,
thy faith and unbelief.

And sorrow, that can kill thee at the kernel,
spares never me, whose sentience is eternal.

1940 (?)

Birth Is
Farewell

1944

Magnet
FOR A.

By what swung hand shall I be hurled
beyond the lode lines of the world
so hard and high that I shall race
on a strict journey into space
forever, and not warp my road
by my own heart's retarding load
into an earth-returning track?
Death, fling me far. Love, pull me back.

1943 (?)

Pattern on File

Under the breaking paper bones of leaves
the bones of mice lie filed in little graves,
record on record. Under the bones of mice,
in pockets indexed by the riding ice,
lie diagrams of lizard, fern in plan,
blueprint of ape, compendium of man.

Fall, 1943

Man in His New Dimension

How many narrowed eyes of boys now brighten
thunder. How many skeletons hurry
through air. How many faces,
whittled by speed and candor, cleave the wind.
Man has become an arrow. He aims himself
high from earth's bow. Wingsperm is in his marrow.

Men are in the cloud, not angels, not the proud
impoverished gods, but men who, hung in peril,
quarrel to end all quarrel, die for life,
battle for peace: man's shadow on the sky
projected from the tribal hearth of earth.

Each mother's son is spurner of the slow
centripetal globe for widening arcs of flight.
Equal to terror now, he climbs the sides
of space, with only one quick downward look for love,
then all his nerves reserved for the huge tides
of time and weather. The earthborn takes his leave
of earth and does not drown in the sky's wave.

1942

I, Adam

I. The Word Was with God

Man jets his image even on my sleep
and calls that God which is his own black shape.

And I am better spoken in the eye
of hawk or bull or fish or the finch's flash.

See with what tact the cat walks, or the fox
winds skeins of scent in the wind.

The leaves are of my mind, pliant in air,
and not defiant of the year's great wheel.

Man, only, makes his wail against my law.
Added, he spoils my sum. I shall subtract him.

II. And Is Renewed with Man

I, Adam, alone, can pace back from myself,
see my own nature, and so thrust beyond it
both ways, to heaven and hell. I, Adam, alone,
have no circumference to keep my bounds
eternally pertaining to my seed
like tree, or guinea hen, or gull, or bear.
I, alone, open in a widening arc,
hopeful of wings, of peace, of resurrection.
I, Adam, have built my Father many mansions
and many images of day and night.

I made the jeweled tabernacle, domes
breast-shaped, and spires evolved to swords of Christ
from phalli that to spur the hesitant wheat

I chiseled huge for awe. I cut my heart
alive from Abel's breast on Aztec towers
and flung it for a sacrifice. I hollowed
the halls of hell under the branching stone
and flame of glass that walled the shouting choirs.

I gave God, who was motherless, a Virgin
to be His Mother, cloaked with the folded sky,
then spiked Him to a tree that She might weep
my sorrow for Him and my self-despisal.

I spitted crying lambs on staffs of gold
and babes on bayonets, that I might probe
chasms of anguish roaring at His heel.

I have made martyrs in His name, and peeled
their skins from them like bloody shirts. I have made
hovels to breed in, and brothels for intricate lusts,
and prisons to go mad in, all in haste
of learning who I am, Who is my Father.

The rapid daggers of the tiger's foot
in me are split: thumb-screw and anaesthetic,
torture and mercy, therefore hell and heaven.
But for the tiger only moon and sun.

Or only hunger and a belly full.

Shall circling hawk be freed from the hawk's ring?
Shall ram surpass his horns, or cat create
more than her litter, or shall the rabbit coin
more than the little copies of herself
to teem her warren and coat my peltless child?

Can the crab, sidling in the jasper sea,
know his own crusted beauty? Can the ape
see his deficiency, or stretch his skull
open to Mozart or the smile of Christ?

What if the ivory diagrams of deer,
their skeletons, are lovelier than fanes
shining in groves of olive or of elm,
articulate with porch or peristyle?
Do the deer know this inward architecture,
and can their thought leap elsewhere from that footing?

The bird has in his seed the fruit of wings,
beak, talons, feathers, the horizoned egg,
and annual, patterned flight, the nest and song.
All these he has, and keeps them in their noose
contained for his bird's purposes; but I
have in my sperm a scope beyond my need,
to know desire beyond each satisfaction,
so that each granting brings a new request.

The wheel was not enough to set me free,
nor fire, nor the harsh arrow, nor the harp,
nor commerce, nor the laws of Archimedes,
nor Euclid's measure, nor the microscope,
nor wings of metal in the shrunken sky.

If I were finite I could speak the word
telling my doom. But I am infinite,
and have not grown the doom yet, nor the tongue.

Early 1943

Eros Out of the Sea

The sleepless ghost perpetually striving
out of the mythical and the actual foam,
Venus and the invertebrate contriving
to make the dry land and the air their home,
obscure their own statistics. Does all vigor
climb from a sea-shell to a cindered star?
Who can tell me, while the spine grows bigger,
what the intention and the limits are?

Toward a faint mark at the far side of dying
see how the boy spins upward from his own
wet element of dream and, suddenly crying,
sets his finned foot upon the arid stone.
Does the child's body, like a luminous symbol,
bottle the marvel, make the boundary tight
and absolute? But childhood, small as a thimble,
looses its genie to the ends of night.

1943

Guilt

A ditch of muddy water; children thrown
into that pit to drown; the water hedged
thick with cold muzzles aimed by mindless boys
who act upon the cog of a command.
This is in Poland. While the children drown,
mothers and fathers hear them and go mad.

This is in Poland. This is in the world.
This is eternal. It cannot be erased.
The guilt of it curves outward in a tide
rushing at England, flooding over France,
roaring upon America. Canute
forbade the waters. But the waters came.

1939–40

The Help Is in You

The emergency is eternal.
Do not cry to me for help!
These tens of thousands weep and die,
but millions died before without my comfort.
Those millions wept and died,
but millions shall die tomorrow without my knowledge.

I can help you, but not today.
I can help you, but not in a thousand years.
I can help you, but not with a check.
I can help you, but you will not be helped.

Weep, O my brothers and sisters!
For death is certain.
Have courage, O my brothers and sisters!
For death shall not be escaped.
Rejoice, O my brothers and sisters!
For the emergency lasts forever.

Hear the alarm! Hurry! Be your own heroes!
You can choose between good and evil.
You cannot choose to live.

1941

High Tide

The leaf is wonderfully veined
but what I love about the leaf
is not its image, but its art
of metaphor. Itself is brief

but through its sunlit tissues, stained
with phantoms of a greener tide,
eternal oceans wash the heart
and monstrous fishes shine and glide.

1943

Sister Arachne

The moth-wing flicks the silver nerve
electric to the spider's brain.
With quick precision to preserve,
the spider winds her net of pain.

The aery cook, her curing done,
hangs up her game in truss of silk.
And she shall have her venison
and I shall have my veal and milk.

1941 (?)

Lamp

The paper that I write upon
wrinkles and withers like a leaf.
The pen is rusting as I write.
The ink is browning. Faint and brief
are the lines I bleed to make.
They'll be rubbed forever soon.
Only the light that pours upon me
its imperishable noon
shall not dwindle where it falls
through and through these blistering walls.

1942

Know What You Do

*Written after Reading the Autobiography
of Ernst Toller*

Yes, it is I who in the verminous cell
hang grey and heavy from the ragged noose
tied out of strips of blanket. I could not stand
the waiting for your coming. It is death
always—sooner or later. If I went
a little way to meet it, that was pride.

And it is I (you need not turn away)
who come at morning on the long green tide
and nudge the shore until the dropping waves
leave me like kelp among the crockery
of rattling sea-shell. Burn me like a branch
of driftwood. There'll be rainbow in the flame.

And when in terror's name you point your gun
level among the others at the wall
where a doomed doll stands staring for his cue,
waiting your chorus for his dance and bow,
know what you do. Remember. It is I.

And it is I who on the callous road
lie felled by emptiness. These are my eyeballs
which glare from their starved caverns. Do not hate them.
They are my eyes that only yesterday
saw the tormenting promise of your coming
with bread and mercy. That you came too late
was not your fault. Need I have doubt of that?

Only, I beg you: do not look away.
This is no strange cadaver. It is I.

November (?), 1943

New England Scrap Heap

We've combed a tangle of iron out of our woods,
out of our fields, our attics, our barns and sheds:
battered ovens, axeheads, rusted plowshares.

We've piled up kiddie kars and dry brown tines
of delicate hayforks; we've reeled up the wires
that marked the lines of our lands, in awkward skeins.

They make a metal scramble near the church,
a pretty heap of history. Our children
slept, sometime, on those beds. Without much search

you'll find the rim you creaked on when you carried
hay to the barn, or maybe the kettle and skillet
your mother spared for you when you were married.

Well, here it is, under the quiet spire.
It might be suitable to say a prayer:

God, if some fragment of my rusted bed
should blast the young bone of some German head,
may the boy sleep. I wish him a long night, curled
in a long dream of a more kindly world.

1942

Back Country

Vermont Intelligence

These hills that lift about us are not walls.
They are a denser sky, a leap of flame
that, flickering in the wind, lets in the world.

Hear in this valley of corn the slip of breech-bolts
quick over grasshopper clack and cricket racket.
Farmers in State Guard khaki, Thursday nights,
wriggle through stubble for attacks on haystacks.

Trains lance the night with hurrying freight of war.
Low bombers wake the cows, shake down the leaves.
The beacon wakes the cocks and scythes the sky.

The postmistress sorts airplanes at the Post.
The Ladies' Guild reels tattle and rolls gauze.
The local aliens, Hitler-haters, blush
under the cold herd-glance of native eyes.

The women pay their men away like coins.
Schoolgirls cry proudly for boys gone. Old men
remember to remember older wars.

The children outline Europe on the blackboard,
chalk a Czech village red, then hurry out
to march beneath the white cone of the church.

These mountains are not walls. These roads are not
roads for escaping. We are not asleep.

Summer, 1942

That Time of Year

As personages, now, the trees emerge
out of anonymous green, each one a forge
that stands in its own color and burns large.

August could scarcely tell sumach from maple,
birch from oak and larch, or beech from popple.
Now no two maples, even, are a couple.

Each is a seraph in his own degree
of gold. He claps his wings in the keen day
and has no peer under the autumn sky.

Verity of the self is only plain
in variation from environs. Green
summer sucks the individual in.

So does white December. Shortly now
these egos shall retreat, resigned to go
into the cold incognito of snow.

Early fall, 1942

Afternoon of a Grown-up

All through the fissures of the colored rocks
the cry rings, the long shrill cry.
Somewhere amongst the hepaticas and flax
childhood is lost and watching, but I lie
looking disconsolate into a mountain pool
at the crowned and crying visage of a fool.
I remember the fawns' hooves, the white
toss of unicorns in woods of morning,
the blue light on crows' backs, the late
tarnish of sunset in a child's sleep-hating eye,
the pity of birds' heads turning
away from me and all my proffered crusts.
And I recall the pricking of all thrusts
against a child's self-love. But I recall
that I was Echo then, not Jonquil,
and ranged the hills, and rang up the blue wall
of thought, and was not anchored to one pool,
however flowered, or tranquil.

April 6, 1942

The Apparition

All is prepared in darkness. Enormous light
is but the foetus of big-bellied night.
The image hatches in the darkened room:
the cave, the camera, the skull, the womb.
Future and past are shut. The present leaps:
a bright calf dropped between two infinite sleeps.

1943 (?)

Residue

The gold breasts of the orange grove
hung amorous to the day's hard love.
I, who am about to die
tomorrow or another day,
remember how the burning fruit
hung heavy downward to the root.

You aimed the camera and took
the ikon of my instant look.
You rolled the image on the reel.
You turned upon your living heel.
I followed to the car. We drove
seaward along the moving grove.

The camera saw the morning plain.
The same gold morning lit your brain.
Only the small grey prints remain.

1943 (?)

Snow

I

Millionfold
now the cold
hexagon
falls upon
iron ground
with no sound.

II

Molecules
follow rules
keeping shy
of the eye.
Water, warm,
shows no form.
Snow, contrarily,
holds less charily
heaven's plan
safe from man.

III

Arithmetic,
numbered thick,
multiplies
to the eyes
beauty built
small as silt,
light as breath,
stiff as death:
crystal angles,
Euclid spangles;

on the tree
jewelry,
on the pond
diamond,
on the glass
flowers, grass,
every bract
made exact.

IV

Number brought
out of nought
must escape
into shape,
must reveal
digit, wheel,
woman, disc,
asterisk,
puma, squid,
pyramid,
serpent, fir,
cylinder.
So the snow,
swirling low,
scatters form
from the storm:
every flake
new of make,
every star
singular.

Early 1942

The Wild Bird

All birds that fly and fall
to claw of cat, or gun, or grief of cage,
cry through my thought: we too, my dear, shall die.

Life is not willing to be clipped of wing
too long, but prisoned small
from reachless frontiers to a cage's size,
ceases at last to drink or sing
and in a lonely rage
breaks through the bars, and flies.

Nothing is still: not thought, not light, not stone.
Even the stiff wings on the floor have flown.

Early 1941

Debris

Do you remember what they sang—
the rose girl and the man of plaster?
Thick with love the gardens hang.
The birds sing disaster.

A time bomb grows among the tulips.
The little mice have gone stone-blind.
There's poisoned sugar in the juleps.
The millionaire has lost his mind.

Where are the lovers, what their harms?
They're just as much in love, and more so.
But the rose girl has lost her arms.
The plaster man has lost his torso.

1942 (?)

F.F.V.

Advertisement

Stand by the heirloom highboy
(with the original handles),
looking the charming hostess
in the flattery of candles.

Privileged, proud and regal,
free from the vulgar fret,
stand there, Junior Legal,
smoking a cigarette.

Stand, busy beauty, keen
on interior decoration,
fox-hunting, being seen
by all the peeping nation.

Stand exquisite and brash
in your frock like a fresh zinnia—
bartered, poor white ash
of a burnt-out Virginia.

Early 1941

The Fools of Evil

The earth beneath the feet of evil men
is chambered with their death.
The deep night of their stealth is webbed with stars
to pry their acts from secrecy. A moon
that tells us of a sun still great in heaven
publishes the deception of their shades.

1941–43

To a Killed Civilian

But it is only death. No further harm
can come to you. The circle is intact.

The slack mouth will not clamp again in pain,
the eyes not fight at opening from sleep,
the mind not crack with horror, nor the loins
cry with the bitter thirst of loneliness.

The utmost mercy has you in its hand.
It even hides from you the way your blood
seeps from the broken flagon of your lungs
like wasted wine along the echoing street.

      Nothing makes the heart
indifferent to death but death itself.

1943 (?)

The Tall Tower

I go to the tall tower.
By its sudden side
life is not heightened,
death is not denied.
But the view widens
and the star comes down
and the separate houses
are a single town.

1943 (?)

To a Mathematician

Whether our messengers be angels or angles,
only intangibles at last are true.
I cannot climb up by your stairs of number
to truth. I use the flight of words, my symbols.
But at the top I think we both must find
what needs no abstract to be understood:
the look of love. And if you have not learned
what love means, then you cannot understand
what I mean either. You have infinity
and I have love. Trust me, they are the same.

1941

Migrants

Birds whose punctual airways
are stairways north and south
expand their small strong lungs
to climb those annual rungs.

Before the northern growth
is green within the eye
those treaders of the sky
have wheeled to wintry earth.

They crack the brown seed-cases
of grasses, goldenrod,
last season's black-eyed Susans.

In dozens and in hundreds
with single kindred motion,
angled in intuition,
they swoop to snatch their ration
upon their northward path.

I did not know the meadow
all widowed of its green
had quite so full a pantry
for quite so many lean
invaders of my country.

Early 1942

Fugue in a Field

In building and breaking of dance, brown mare,
black gelding, lift and fall in a field in a
battle of contacts and tangents.

With plangence of neighing, in furious, amorous
fettle, they rock to a pattern of playing forever
set down by the lion and unicorn trying their
mythical mettle all round the town.

Hocks interlock, knees knock, necks arch, tails
curve in braiding of nerve, muscle, mind—a
tussle and wrestle designed for the badge of a shield.

Not cattle, not men, could fence with a rhythm so
subtle, but streams of two waters that clash and
entwine, or themes of a fugue both in league and at
war in debate of design.

Early 1942

Note to Charles Darwin

Sorrow took the swinging ape
and twisted it to human shape.

1941

The Little Bright One

Where the little
bright one runs
sparks fly.
He has the sun's
fire in his feet
and where he sprints
all the stones
are flints.

1942

The Dark Room

The camera takes and locks what paleolithic man
took deep in eye and mind and imaged on the rock.

He worked with ochre, remembered with his hands
the hunted creature for the future hunter.

The lens can isolate the static look
of horses' necks and hocks at a section of speed,
but not more candidly than did the eye
of Adam's grandchild in the stifling cave.
By firelight out of bowls of bison fat
he crushed the oxide ore and drew on the flickering dome
the mammoth charging, the reindeer with his head
turned back in lovely awkwardness to hear
some alien tumult in the unseen thicket.

The naked man, whose brother nicked from stone
weapons for battle and cattle killing, worked
impassioned and absorbed, and scattered thick
in the brain-cells of the race the Sistine seed.

We think of the nations of the painted rocks
as wakers in the shambling dawn of thought.
They may as well have been the residue
of wrecked economy, vestigial peoples
who banked within the persons of their artists
immortal fires of intellectual force.

The mind spins backward, fainting, to that time
before our Christ and after other christs
and finds the substance of both art and life
tougher than imagination, surpassing thought,
establishing the eternity of the world
that rises and crumbles forever in restless apparition

and ceaseless disappearance; the plastic humus
that sun and faith and sexual desire
diversify into forests, towers and children.

Early 1943

Not According to Plan

The seed is final and compact,
the premise is without a flaw,
but from the stripped and frozen fact
a crooked truth is made to thaw.

Observe that while the theorem
predicts a strict and crystal shape,
the flower struggles from the stem
in asymmetrical escape.

1943

Elegy for an Engineer

To the Memory of My Father

I

The lees of flesh, the white and stubborn dregs
of bones that stood for nearly sixty years
right-angled to the magnet of the grave,
are boxed in blackness. Some six pounds of ash
that choked the mouth of fire and were rejected
lie under fern. There on a summer day
after long rain I walked and was confounded
to find trout lily, trillium, partridge berry
drawing green tissue over the earth's wound,
while new pines moved in a contracting ring
like waters closing over a small island
to drown it from the eye and from the mind.

Down on my knees! Till then I had not known
how strong my fingers were to tear at roots
and turn a tide. Wiser perhaps to yield
to time and trees and let the flood engulf
grief and remembrance and the senseless ash.
But I had brought you flowers, and a vine
strong to encroach upon the primitive moss
and push weeds backward with a thought of gardens.

II

Man is a spirit. Let the priest declare
body and ghost as pitched in endless fight.
I have learnt well how swiftly on the air
the tactual image is erased from sight.
Only a pulse ago your shape was there
that now has gone. I go to the shut grave
and find that, though your look and speech remain

sharp in my blood and constant in my brain,
your body was as transient as a wave.

III

Flesh is a traveller, but the soul grows roots.
Your mind shaped matter to endure in space
as buildings that displace the actual air
and give intangible time a spine of stone.
The parallelogram, the cone, the sphere,
geometry projected into use,
stand for their instant in eternal flux:
your signature upon the sensory world.

Here are the tools, the delicate, vast machines,
the brain's auxiliaries to the limited hand,
the artisan in metal multiplied.
These mills fulfill the contract of your thought
with your brief days to add an excellence
of matter and knowledge to the peace of men.
Here's your creation.
                        If you should return
in wish or specter out of death's abstraction,
you would not come to us, who loved and love you,
but to appraise the fiber of these works,
to walk among the timed, industrious thunders
of your prescription, through these obdurate halls
in Florida flatlands or northwestern valleys,
where water fit for harness, trees for felling,
happened together.
                        You would walk your bridges
to test their tension under a ghost's weight,
and mark the responses of a natural force
to supernatural energies. You'd jot
huge mathematics on a plane of light
to contradict the counsel of despair
that human lines are parallel, shall never
meet again, even beyond the farthest star,

and prove, while Euclid's castles in the ether
crash to the relative earth, and Einstein fiddles,
that ultimately parallels may touch.

IV

On a clear morning I should like to take
your tripod, set an eye against the lens,
and see if the thin cross of spider threads
could mark the spot you stand on. Yet I know
how blunt this instrument of earthly survey
would be to trace you in your new dimension.

Not through the eye of the theodolite
shall I assess your harsh removal from us.
Only, perhaps the telescope shall turn
to childhood and the valleys that you showed us
into whose basins you would pour aside
rivers to turn pine forests into lakes,
or lakes you'd empty dry, and land reclaim
out of the barren keeping of the sea.

If I could set my foot upon a bridge
of your design, and cross the computed river
to find myself not on the anchored bank,
but in an hour unclocked, a space unreckoned,
might I not then past deafness hear your voice
and beyond blindness see you walking towards me
affectionately, as you used to come,
with old jests and unaging joy in work?

V

The child climbs out of evening, out of ruin
into a green morrow. His mind, spooled small,
is a new watch-spring, coiled to the click of time,
wound by our stubborn hope to keep forever
our flashing minute.

The child wades through a rising tide of grass.
I walk in the thin wake,
a stain of trodden stalks. He does not see
the track behind him, sliding back to me,
nor know that through my life his heels shall leave
that bruised and silver clue.

I shall so often trace him—over acres
swelling with all the seed of his next summer.
Leaves that shall cluster green above his head
shall where I follow lie in fallen gold,
while, driven on, with backward-glancing eyes
of pity and impatience and remorse,
he'll without haste exceed me and my love,
and leave me only phantoms of the self
he was each moment past. Birth is farewell.
When he was born I lost him to the future.
But, though his pace be swift to carry him
out of my eyes, a frail track shall persist
as if a snail had crept.

The narrow track, the thread, the silver cord,
trembles through time, always at point to break
by death or anger, but the taut line holds.
Father to daughter, mother to son, it runs
through night and day forever. In this boy
your eyes rekindle, and you stand again
to the hard challenge of the hindered task.

Often I watch him and believe he strives
to make his unaccustomed flesh remember
old skills that you and all his ancestors
practiced before him—to recall a pattern,
a music of the sinews, a design
of mind and nerve in intricate counterpoint.

It is as if he listened for a cue
more than we can provide him. And at times

he hears it, and his prentice face is lit
with the long recollection of the race.

This child, the latest flower of a seed
cast before reckoned time in clay wrung clean
by cataclysm in the fluid rock,
is your light link of nerve and curious thought
with all the valiant failure of the world.

VI

O Love! In what secret closets of forever
we lock your images from rust and fading.

How, sentenced, we conspire to baffle death
with all the careful windings of our vows.

And to what small avail we utter: Always!
against the noise of nothing's climbing wave.

O Love! For all our protest, when that wave
is reeled back by the sea in lapsing thunder,
we hear the one word: Hush.

1940–42

Northwest

With keen and crystal keys of death
the mountains lock the sky and plain.
The skiers with their clouding breath
drop and climb, drop and climb.

The peaks are pointed out of time
and grappled to no human pain.
Diminished to a cricket's chime
is all that man can say or do.

I have not looked on day so blue,
a sun so brilliant on the brain
to prick the eye and pierce it through
with beauty clean of overtones.

There's little heartbreak in these zones,
or guilt in all this pure terrain,
or residue of Adam's bones
under the unhistoric stones.

December 23–27, 1941

The Little Girls

The eyes of the little girls are lit with projects
like windows honey-gold at edge of night.
The little girls are houses, swept and dusted,
busy and sane and proud with purposes.

I was a child who clutched the amulet
of childhood in a terror of time. I saw
archangels, worshipped trees, expected God.

The heavens of these children are within their reach.
Sweeping their elders' floors, they dream of love.

When Bertha tells me with a crystal smile
that Girl Scouts meet on Friday; when Kathleen
boasts that she's learning how to bake at school;
when Betty, making beds, fattens the pillows
with confident hands, I marvel and look back
at scented cedar pagodas ringed around
the solitary spirit of a child
who like a spindly deer ran from the trap
of house and hurried up the nearest slope
to push the horizon out and keep time still.

I love these girls as we can only love
what is mysteriously different from us.
I was the flare that cools into a poet.
They are the earth that every turning spring
breaks through the snow and branches into a world.

1942–43

Nautilus

Let the mind compel
what the veins wish
and shape a cool shell
round the coiled fish,

but let the pearl case
have a stair that turns
from the secret place
to the sea ferns.

1941 (?)

Mrs.

The gentle matron watches me with eyes
like two brown sherries. She is not impelled
to more than vague misgivings or surmise
by my smooth manner and my hand outheld.

What can she value that I have to yield?
She asks no more elation for her blood
than to prepare forever the same field
in the eternal kitchen of the cud.

1942

The Sheathed Anger

All who love each other
walk in the green woods
delicately away
from the cruel sportsmen.

They do not look for death.
They look for life
and they wear trees of horn
proudly like crowns
on their balanced heads.

Peace is their food,
and grass and all quiet things
their grace.
But hard in the herd
as veins of diamond
the unreckoning valor
of the angry buck.

November, 1941–January 20, 1942

Physic for Madness

The weapons are dipped in venom. The eternal phantoms
of man and man are locked again in fury.
Men hate each other because they hate themselves.
They long to smash the images of God
which are themselves, forgetting that death will end
the matter soon enough. And so they hit
brother at brother in mutual disgust.

What First Aid can I give till the Doctor comes?
I could give you God, but God in this clever age
is out of favor with society—
a Common Person, a Jew. And we no longer
call on him. Nevertheless he is at home
all week, not only on Sundays.

Truth I could recommend, or charity, but these
are tenuous virtues with no market value.
However, I have a possible prescription:

I give you the vision of death. If every man
remembered every day that he must die,
he would not break his heart for power or money,
but break it up as bread and give it away.

1943 (?)

Yggdrasill

A POEM FOR ODELL WALLER*

I, groping home through darkness, saw a tree.
It writhed against a heraldry of worlds
and grasped the planet with its nervous roots.

On such a tree Christ hung. Out of such wood
cold punishment or hot reprisal shape
gallows or lynch-tree, reckoning white or black.

Upon such boughs against the zodiac
I too am pendant. Through my crookèd hands
grind constellations. Under my nailed feet
the muddy pools are shaken with thrown stars

that wake among the hates of white men's justice.

1942

---

* Oscar Davis, a poor and debt-ridden white man, was shot on July
15, 1940, by Odell Waller, his Negro share-crop tenant, for refusal
to give up Waller's share of their wheat crop. Convicted by an all-
white jury which included ten share-crop operators, Waller was condemned to death. His case was fought for two years through the
Virginia and Federal courts by persons who believed it symbolic of
the evils, to both whites and Negroes, in the share-crop and poll-tax
systems. The defense contended mainly that Waller had not been
tried by a jury of his peers. Governor Darden granted him five stays
of execution, but refused a sixth.
Waller was put to death on July 2, 1942.

Alter Ego

Where did I go amiss? I drew a line
straight as a shaft of starlight—so I thought—
to be the certain index of my life.
But the beam struck some accidental glass
that sent it wide and pointed me to this:
the weirdly damaged one with whom I live
too intimately all my days, whose eyes
meet mine in mirrors, and whose sudden tongue
speaks words I would not dream.

Early 1942

Advice to Heroes

We are grooming you now for wounds we can't kiss better.
The iodine bottle and the Band-Aid box,
the chair-leg scolded when you barked your shins,
are grown inadequate, ridiculous,
measured beside your valor, our remorse.

We are sending you off to school to learn our lesson.
Good-bye. Be good, and bloody. Be quick to unlearn
all that we taught you out of our ignorance:
tolerance, temperance, mercy. Thou shalt not kill
anyone but the enemy. That is to say
our enemy, for if indeed you killed your own
you might turn back and strangle most of us.

Early 1943

Eye Strain

I can't read on a train.
The words are Humpty-Dumpty
that neither horse nor man can put together.
Also, my thoughts are thrown forth by the journey
out of their center. Time and space are flattened
by the wheeled speed against my meteor face.

I can't read in this room.
The words are smeared to nonsense.
I thought a poem might afford me peace
or faith or courage. But the print is blurred:
the planet shakes so much.

Early 1942

The Gentled Beast

At the kiss of my heel,
at the flex of my wrists,
he rears, resists
the signs of my will.

He balks, he tugs the rein,
dances to throw me.
I master him. He must show me
the size of his disdain.

In fugue of flesh and mind
we fight, and are conjoint:
hard counterpoint
contending to one end.

He must yield. When my finger
feels a mouth of feather,
and my boot's leather
bears on his flank no stronger

than a windblown seed,
only then shall he race
reinless, at his own pace:
a speed beyond my speed.

September, 1942

The Cruellest Month

The rites of April shake the light with grief
and exaltation. The perennial pyre
scorches staked dryads with green fire of leaf.
Half-gods are changed to martyrs in that fire.
Trees put aside their innocence and grow
a Christian fortitude of sacrifice:
invert Sebastians wounded from the pith
by buds that choose a target in the sun.
That god was slaughtered. He must perish twice
and many times and sleep beneath the snow
until he break it with the fact and myth
of Easter's crocus. Now that rivers run
not alone over bedrock, not alone
of water, sliding headlong and oblique
downward from watersheds, but vertical
through branchèd fiber skyward, now we speak
of spring that with our longing has enticed
Persephone from her marriage bed in Hell,
has cracked Osiris from his painted shell
and from the stony grave has startled Christ.

1943 (?)

Image in Empty Water

The river runs as brown as ale.
I learnt its meaning in no school.
To my five senses, none the less,
it tells a truth I cannot miss
and half can speak. Although I look
under the fern, under the rock,
through their reflections, all I learn
is: clear as water I was born,
void as the river, cold as the river
running out of rock forever.

When to my banks you walk, to stand
looking within to see beyond,
looking within for truth or love,
I cannot give more than you give.
Your image trembles in the stream.
All that you haunt me with, I am.

1942

Last of Phantasy

Long enough now the shadowless unicorn
has trod no hoofprints into rootless flowers.
1 have been shouted awake in a loud wood
where hemlocks roar their black tides at the sun
out of the clefts of the unconscious rock.

Deception of the tapestry is this:
it has not, stitched beneath its thousand flowers,
the whiff and dampness of last autumn's ruin;
has not the menace of the noise of water
loosing the stones all down the dwindling mountain.

My unicorn, whose sides were bright as nothing,
dries like a teardrop in the actual sun,
and there an old bear, stinking and opaque,
roars drunken sleepy from his frowsy bedroom
and drives me, sweating, through the terrible trees.

1943

Lot's Daughter

You, being grown and little pleased by growth,
look back to childhood with an envious eye
that sees no snare in the remembered heath,
no shadow in the clockless golden day.

You see your yesterday self: why-saying child
armed with enchanted formulae direct
from servants' tongues or books whose words were spelled
trustingly into thought, then into act.

Time is illumined with inverted light:
the past all whole, the present weird with fault.
Look back no more. The child's eyes burn with hate
watching the woman harden into salt.

1943

Vision of Peace

The Lord my God has retinas of distance.
I stood at his eye's lash and saw forever.

The Lord my God has tympanums of silence.
I listened at the chambered drum, the door
clattered by chaos and the brassy stars,
by choirs, artillery, mundane seas and winds,
sidereal tides, the pulses of a mouse,
and all that noise lay faint as household dust
on a washed window.

The Lord my God puts halt upon my haste
with one calm counsel: Do not move so quickly,
pricked by your little term. In me there's time
and room for all requitals.

1942

The Fall

At the world's end the world shall look like this:
black trees consumed with fire, and burning bushes;
brown paper leaves, curled brittle, blown abroad;
parched ferns, and failing flame of goldenrod
blazing an instant more before its ashes
float nowhere through a starry rain of ice.

1942

There's Time Enough

There's time enough: an afternoon or forever,
an aeon of fern or an instant of revelation.

1943 (?)

Green Guest

Has the old man mislaid his childhood?
Has he forgotten the green boy?

A pine tree, like a history,
testifies with hardening records
to a series of attempts.

The soft pale needles, like new teeth,
push the dark ones to the ground.

Transient inhabitant, the dryad
is locked within the ageing fiber
and the old man when he dies
sets a child free on the wind.

1943 (P)

Song Before Peace

Now the birchtree, shaken and tatterskinned,
springs, packed with leaf, against a slow wet wind,

having all winter long leaned with a wind that laid
feathers of ice against its other side.

Now the sumach pours its metal veins
in moulds of air to make its buds of bronze.

Now tongues of light cry April in the mind.
Wounds heal to leaves along the heart's brown rind.

And the felled willow, the split tree of man,
lifts wands of yellow to the mounting sun.

April–May, 1943–January 6, 1944

Small Elegy

For your sake
we shall not break
the winter ground.
The flesh of the dead
is fishes' bread.
Sleep a deep sleep,
O valiant drowned!
Sleep sound.

1941

Ten Leagues Beyond the Wide World's End

I pursue him, the loved one all unsolved,
through mines of mercury, salt caves and folded stone,
down decimal steps of dream and sleep and death,
through flowering, breaking rocket-head of war
and long anxious ferment of peace.

I pursue him whom I might catch if ever
only by sitting still.
I know, I have taken with sliding rule and wavering scale
his height and shape not fixed but leaping and falling
like fire and shadow forever between child and man.
I know his voice, treble and bass, infantile and mature.
I know the chords of his changes from god to demon
within the scale of his humanity.

I think he is my lover or my child.
When I attempt to take him in my arms
he pulls away from me with a boy's pride
and walks to the edge of the burning world with a gun in his hand.

Early 1944

Mine, But Not to Keep

FOR EACH OF THREE, A, E, AND D

Whenever I leave you, it is good night forever.
Whether in dream or waking I see your eyes
I have not seen them before. They are unknown
as wrapped gifts. And I fall at once in love
over and over again. Tissue by tissue, I tear
the strangeness off until I find the center
that every time is you and every time is mine.
I cannot tire of you. I cannot keep nor use you,
but only find and lose you, again and again.
Stranger, it is my love that holds you new,
that saves you from the tarnish of its keeping.
Whether awake or sleeping, whenever I see you
it is good morning. It is for the first time.

Early 1944

Walk
Through
Two
Landscapes

1949

"Each man from his lost afternoon,
from the far landscape of his yearning
seeks in the focused symbol of return
the nucleus of time
within one tense."

Monica Roberts Chalmers

Ego

Ego

Vague, submarine, my giant twin
swims under me, a girl of shade
who mimics me. She's caught within
a chickenwire of light that's laid
by netted waves on floor of sand.
I dare not look. I squeeze my lids
against that apparition and
her nightmare of surrounding squids,
her company of nounless fright.
She is the unknown thing I am
and do not wish to see. In flight
I swim the way my comrades swam
and hide among them. Let me keep
their safety's circle for a charm
against that sister in the deep
who, huge and mocking, plans me harm.

Summer, 1948

New Leaf

I beat, I beat upon the tightened drum.
The skin of it has a familiar smell.
It smells of me. It makes a mighty sound.

I ring, I ring the ancient rowdy bell.
The tongue of it has a familiar taste.
It tastes of mine. It rings for miles around.

I run, I run to every house but mine,
but as the door swings open, there I stand
in hateful welcome, and invite me in.

I shall stay here and ring no bell and beat
no drum, but wait, and see who runs to me,
who rings, who beats, and see what may begin.

1948 (?)

Rescue

A creature comes to me. His paws are fire.
My nerves become a tree of lighted wire
charging the mind with life when he is near.

If he come down from God or out of hell
there is no brand upon his hide to tell.
Simply, I know that he is wonderful.

He fades back to his ambush of cool leaves
and all is safe. And I am empty. Doves
conduct a Quaker life beneath my eaves

until their dogma lulls me to despair.
The leaves move. There's the leopard! At his roar
the doves snow upward in the crazy air.

1945 (?)

Ocean Fable

There is a fish
whose anus is his mouth.
In his beginning is his end.
He is his own foe and friend

and the reply to his own wish.
This creature of primeval mud
is born forever in the blood.
But higher up, in swifter tides,

the murderous swordfish stabs and slides.
They say the complex octopus

is subtly brained and amorous.
I, tidal in my acts and wishes,

perceive how hierarchies of fishes
kill and make love in me. My God,

grant me the rage of shark or cod
but mark my exits, one for dung,

another for the mind and tongue,
and let the fish whose shape is O
cease breeding self in night below.

Summer, 1945

Ordeal of the Cave

I am the mother of Aladdin. I
have a young son who must explore the cave.
I cannot go with him where all that brave
damnation shines, those spurious treasures lie.
I'll have no talisman to cheer him by
when the rubbed bronze that failed to bring the slave
reeks of snuffed wick; and, like an oily wave,
the jewels heave and vanish at his cry.

Down through that magic he must plunge, to climb
out of its hold. I stand aside, and trust
that when the waking hurts him, as it must,
he'll find what I have found in my own time:
strength in the bitter rock, life in the slime,
and brilliant universes in the dust.

1946 (?)

Only the Root

I am sorry and ashamed. I am ashamed
both of the evil I have done and of the evil
I have suffered to be done. I think the devil
is a perfect lady elegantly named

with an education and a charming smile
and too much niceness to be coarse, or swear,
or to desire to kill, or break a chair
over some skull whose thoughts she knows are vile.

I'm no such lady, though they planned me so
in early blueprints. Maybe this redeems
me from my ancient guilt: that from my dreams
a spring arises that could someday flow

into the conscious fields, become a flood.
Only the radical might survive that mud.

1947 (?)

Convenient Object

When the axe bit this bronzed tree, it broke gold.
The sweet wood weeps in the sun, its death a fragrance.
The ragged knots which show where boughs were hacked
make me think of knees of spent old horses
picking at hay gone fair and foul with flowers.

I can gaze long and quiet on this corpse
folded in sunlight. Spiders dart across it.
(How quick a spider is when it's not waiting!)
The cut trunk is a hook to haul up thoughts—
drag them from deep, from far, and give them roost.

To the mystic his mandala, to the god his thumbs,
to me this object awkward and evocative,
which if I were a carver I could chip
into a lynched innocent with brow more scored
even than mine, or if my child were cold,
could cut and kindle, or if I were drowning,
could clutch in the mindless stream, or, being as I am,
astray and brooding, can take for handhold, mindhold,
as a thing strong though stricken.

Early 1949

Clear Specter

FOR MONA

Your image lasts as bright
as though you were not dead
nor moved an inch away.
You had no wish to stay
but blundered as you fled
and left yourself in flight.

You are not free even now. Your ghosts are spooled
here in this tomb or womb or picture box
in which your image burns in kodacolor.
You can't sleep yet. It's not the hour for peace.
You dig within my dark, a restless miner
questing the black rock for the brilliant vein,
and you shall quarry yet (O dead too soon!)
out of my loss poems you never wrote.

Junior to me, you could have seen me go
first with more fitness, having come with me
a narrow way for years, looking for truth.
You found it first: that love is strong as death,
death dear as life. For when your child went out
like a small star in heaven, you burned low
and flickered, and were quenched. Two ones make nothing
and nothing everything. You are one fire
that flames now in our thought, you and the child
who said he wished never to be a man
and had his sad wish granted. How your son
became your parent, bearing you to death,
we shall remember always and be quiet
before the mystery of such a love.

Our care was as superfluous as food.
You had your ears cocked for a call outside,

saw how the street that ran beneath the window
might carry you to him, away from us.
You shrugged, slapped, shook us off, and not with hate
but only haste to be off. And we remain,
grieved and offended. How death must have shone
huger than life in your lost eyes to draw you so!

We have lain and walked, since, where your absence
has been a presence. Gone, you come through roofs
like wind, a funneled whirlwind that would draw
the living after you. There's fear in this
that we shall see too soon, before our evening,
that you were right in choosing noon to go.

O bitter girl, gone in the young daylight,
child grown tall, grown ripe, but not grown wise
in our way of wisdom, all our wisdom, then,
was hollow as the house of the hornet.
Death is a better knowledge.

> I sleep. You split my night.
> I wake and taste your death.
> You are not gone so far
> but what you were and are
> is name that begs my breath
> is form that fills my sight.

1946–47

I Wake and Think

I wake and think
how much I love
my loves

how my love's weak
to save them from
all wounds

how my love
cannot last
longer than I

nor can their
having it survive
their deaths.

Our love
dies with us?
Oh—if this be true

death is love's measure.
I cannot sleep. I
cannot sleep.

1947

Tree of Fire

Native to That Place

Men who with wide and narrow eyes
investigate the huge and little
have not been able to devise
lenses to pierce to Paradise.

Apocalypse to any saint
is heaven frescoed in his skull
and the angelic brother's paint
on the cell wall at last grows faint.

Without a crown or telescope
the child who sings because he wakes
inhabits heaven past the hope
of Galileo or the Pope.

1946 (?)

Tree of Fire

Out of the vegetable heart
on ladders of a hidden light
climbs up the blazing tree of art
whose secret boughs of inward sight
ring with the birds of Yeats and shake
with angels of St. John and Blake.

And from those boughs through which no sap
siphons to fall shall fruit be shook
of bronze and ruby to your lap
(there where you sit and skyward look)
which eaten, shall not taint your breath
with appled scent of life and death.

And there beneath those tenting boughs
which are a roof above desire
recall how time was made to house
brute, man, and ghost, how light and fire
were the beginning, were the root
and are the everlasting fruit.

Early 1949

Voyage

Past what peripheries of cloud and star,
across and through what fathoms we keep watch
with mariners' eyes half shuttered by horizons.

Crew of the holystoned globe, with more than the wind
shouting along our shrouds—the hours and ether,
time and infinity in a high, thronging storm—
we sail, and swinging continents of sky
flow round us in their wheel of distances
slowly, as if to bring us through long shoals
to the lost harbor where we cried farewell.

Middle 1940's

They Know Not

O angry gentle man, my comrade Christ!
How you have suffered more than from the driven
metal of malice! Have you yet forgiven
the thieves who, not beside you, not who diced
to take your garments, not the friend who priced
your love in silver, but the thieves of heaven
who filched your meaning, multiplied by seven
the single truth that nourished and sufficed?

Blind to your parable, good people praise
your kitchen prowess: fishes multiplied,
bread squared, and wine for wedding days supplied.
They stumble to you with their breakfast trays
and with a bloody breadknife slice your side,
then go, still famished, on their earthen ways.

Early 1949

When Yellow Leaves . . .

Now in the maple tree the phoenix roosts:
bird of September flame
that shall ignite the landscape. Where he rests
we see the summer dream
curl like a snapshot thrown in the lit hearth—
burnt leaf of the green past.
The phoenix settles in his nest of death
to hatch his holocaust.

September, 1946

Once Upon an Eternity

An angel stood in the sunflooded room beside the bookcase looking at my books.

Hello. Help yourself, I said. Read as many as you like.

Thank you, the angel said. I've just come out of that one. He pointed to *Religio Medici*.

There are others you may not have gone through, I suggested.

Undoubtedly, he replied with a charming smile. But I see through them all. Come with me and I'll show you something more profound.

He led me into the field and gave me a small flower. I realized that I would never learn the language in which it was written but the binding moved me to tears. The angel gently took the flower away and said, Come with me and I'll show you something closer to you.

He took me to where a goat stood throwing back his bearded chin and looking at the world from upside down. Seeing me, the goat gathered himself, rose like a wave and butted me hard. Closer to me, indeed! I thought. He loves you, the angel laughed. Then he said, Come with me and I'll show you something farther from you.

He took me to a garden where a child sat on the grass petting a young wingèd leopard. I sat down and played with the child for several minutes before I realized that it was myself at the age of two. Now come with me, the angel said, and I will show you a thing more wonderful.

He took me to a barn and there on the side of it, on the weather-bleached boards of grained silver, a man was wreathed and crucified. Come with me, the angel said, and I will show you a sadder thing.

He led me to an orchard and told me to look up into an apple tree. There among the fruit I saw growing from one of the branches a human foetus. Look close, the angel said. I looked and saw in the pleated face of the rosepink monkey the foreshadowing of the features of my son.

I turned to the angel and asked, Is there no hope? And the angel said, Break the branch.

As I broke the branch the wings of the angel withered and vanished. The branch faded from my hand and I saw that the angel was my son grown tall.

Your wings! I cried. What has happened to your wings?

He looked over first one shoulder then the other then shrugged them both. Oh, those?

If it's not rubbers or raincoats, it's wings, he muttered. Mother, he said reprovingly, you're always harping on trifles. Do try to leave me alone. I have so much to do.

1945 (?)

Victorian Seraglio

I thumb back to the golden day when Godey
petticoated the parlor, upholstered the Lady,

who, plastroned, hooked, and garlanded with garniture,
was Home Sweet Home's most yielding piece of furniture

if stiffest animal, for Lawks! the pugs
and cats lacked bones. Cherubic on hooked rugs

they gazed at God, and, fat with food and piety,
knew themselves symbols of a blameless laity.

Then, big-eyed little girls in boots and bustles
posed with pet birds near whatnots dripping tassels

and little boys with sailor hats like haloes
shrimped in stiff suits, were shod to wade the shallows.

Wire on the buttocks, buckram at the breast,
then kept the maidens mindful to be chaste

if thoughtful to be wed. But in this pageant
why is the male so absent if so cogent?

We guess him in the condescending stitch
sewn for his sake: the plush tobacco pouch,

the blooming slippers, the newspaper rack
of garnet watered silk, the shaving book

of peacock velvet done in puce chenille:
a Lady's Work. She stitches beads on tulle

and days on nothingness. Pure and polite,
she's insulated from her brutal mate

who sweats profanely just outside the circle
to foot the bills for this Olympian sparkle,

this Cashmere ritual, this sacred frippery
of Goddesses who smite with bolts of drapery.

Who'd trade this whaleboned virtue and gentility
for all of Carrie Chapman Catt's equality?

Now woman's work, like man's, is done the harsh way
by Dorothy Thompson and by Freda Kirchwey.

Oh where are the shows of yesteryear and Godey?
What in the world has happened to his Lady?

Late 1946

Lutesong for Young Angels

To MARY PRAY

Maybe
all Paradise
may be
in May.

Angels on their celestas
could not ping
prettier notes
than small birds sing.

As for jonquils—
painters are great sillies
to paint for Mary's posies
only lilies,

since May is Mary's month—
the month of May
when daffodils wave sunlight
out of clay,

and leaves are infantine
and trees are faintly
haloed with gold
and stand all saintly

with praise of rain
with laud of light
after winter's
woodchuck night.

All things seem to sing
and to clap

at the climbing
of the sap.

With the greening
of the grass
Mary's miracle
comes to pass.

So to Persephone
and Mary pray
and sing and say:
Sorrow away!
All's good that's gay.

Then pluck and play
what time we may.

Maybe
all Paradise
may be
in May.

Early 1949

Delicate Truth

All down the sides of the mind, as down the concave
walls of a sky or bubble, earth's illusion
pours its pictures, its erotic, shining
images of creation, not to be encompassed
by logic, not to be quite defined
by noun or number, but like a host of angels
shyly to be adored by the quick eye
that looks and looks away lest all should vanish
scared and offended by a gross regard.

1948 (?)

Three Times Two

Walk Through Two Landscapes

For Betty Sherrard

We walked together in two different landscapes
sharply refracted through two temperaments.
My scene was huge—compared with yours, austere
and spare of nouns: a study in planes of color,
olive and ivory and violet
slipping away in squeezing parallels,
in long arcs of leave-taking from the eye.

My landscape was a spectrum of my dream
of time and magnitude, and of that point, myself,
that has position but no magnitude.
It was the frail projection of a thought
that for a half-convincing moment filled
the cupped panes of the eyes, the brain's small theater.

And yours: you walked fastidiously. You saw
with eyes half clinical, half amorous,
the intimate anatomy of a season.

Out of the sleeves of summer you perceived
small birds to fly, or what to me were birds,
but what you saw with more particular sight
were waxwing, grosbeak, bobolink or lark;
crested or capped, and whether cock or hen.

For you, no planes of ivory, olive, mauve,
but mouse-moved wheat and siskin-shaken pine,
orchis, erigeron, vervain or vetch.
For you, incarnate species, named like friends,

whose constant presence reinforced your faith
that earth was no illusion, but a fact
older than knowledge, solid beyond sense.

Uneasy in my abstract universe,
I felt my dearth of fact as a defect,
my vision nakedness; yours, rich insignia.
A hundred things occurred in every inch
sprung of their hundred words. A microscope
lived in your pupils. You divined the seed
breaking to tree and flower, while I guessed
energies thrusting through regenerate systems.

Summer, 1944

Dilys Bennett at about age 13

Gray's Harbor, Washington, 1928

Inhuman View

Reaching like foetus hands, wrinkled and pink,
leaves of the maple open all over the hill.
These crumpled nylon births have still upon them
watery skysheen of the recent caul.

Sparse in the rose-fleshed tumult of the maples,
shad bushes splash their sprays of milky stars,
and brooks, tea-colored from their umber gravel
run by roadsides, puckering over stones
in static frills of turbulence, like waves
eternally breaking on a Brueghel sea.

Brueghel and Botticelli. Names of men
lie over landscape. With Perugino's eye
we penetrate a distance, through Cézanne's
prism can break a valley into cubes.
Mozart and Bach have cocked our ear, and Wordsworth
tainted the innocent flora with an ethic,
until we know creation through a mind
weary with thought, sick with mortality.

Yet there are moments when the eyebeam breaks
through memory and sees the utter fact:
earth, bird, or tree, not bird of Paradise
or tree of hell, or earth of history,
but something prior with the dream stripped off.

Where breasts of gravel have been blasted through,
and recent wounds of roadbanks gape to the light,
there the short fringe of roots hangs down and shows
how shallow the verdure, how the garment of spring
is mildew on the antique bone. The skin
of earth lies only inches thick on rock,

chlorophyll smear upon the sterile planet,
the skull of shale, fire, ice, and furtive ore.

There poetry has seldom dug, nor art
meddled, but bald geology has poked
and come up with prodigious mystery
older than greed or mercy, leaves or love.

Summer, 1945—Summer, 1949

Lines on the Sea

The sky's lip and the sea's lip shut in peace.
The horizontal is the line of calm.
Masts move across it: pigmy verticals.
Speeding diagonals of leaning sails
startle awake the eye that's drowsed with trust.
All's well, the horizon says. Peace—peace.
Time and more time is man's, whether for commerce
or purely for being, and knowing that he is.

But there's an unseen perpendicular
from the horizon, and every drowned man slides
down it to such an everlasting peace
as skyline never speaks of to the nerves.
Sane, living men refuse it. Every ship
keeps watch against that hanging rope. The sailor
would rather think the ocean wide than deep.

Thus he moves horizontally. His eyes
narrow for panoramas. His glance goes
laterally, to the land, where verticals
are skyscrapers and silos, towers, trees,
and even the little vertical of man
is blocked out solid in a capital I.

Summer, 1949

Not One Atoll

Not One Atoll

Phi Beta Kappa Ode delivered at Tufts College,
1946

I

Mountains far off are abstract majesty.
Under our feet they are the risen earth.
Even the smallest man may touch the sky
seeing that the sky comes down to him.
The foetus is the prophecy of God,
the attentive heart the crossroads of all myths.
If I had never learned the life of Christ,
as I am a mother I should guess that tale.

History has no shape if it be not man's.
Yesterday is his regret, tomorrow his resolution.
All the tribes of the future use his loins as a road,
use the womb as a tavern. The joy and the guilt
are not gone or to be, but only are
present forever in the present being.
I am. I sin. I love. The delicate scales
teeter upon the cradle of the pelvis.

Generation is the steady beat
on the skin drum in the jungle, the root of music.
The sky shakes and its veils fall into folds
suggesting forms. The forms are born dancing.
The forms are heartless and innocent: flowers, beasts.
When the heart grows, the fatal, passionate fruit,
wickedness breeds. Exasperated fury

of self-disgust puts forth the brilliant flower
of war and murder. Not till man has eaten
his own heart out shall he be cured of grief.

II

I knew as I carried my son in my bursting skin
I was no better than the world. I was indeed the world
carrying its own hope under its strained heart.
The creature woman when she is with child
sees with an ancient introspective eye.
All her webbed nerves perceive what she creates
at the dark center, and the excluded world
of men and politics and war and commerce
is shape and soundtrack on a reeling film.

To the woman who is with child time is nine months long.
And in the ninth month she ends her work which she has made
and is delivered and rests, and sees her work that it is
good, created in the image of herself and of her lord.
And in the stable with the ox and ass
she worships her ugly baby and puts her nipple
between the angry lips of a new nation.

The infant grows. And shall he measure the cross
with his stretched arms, or shall he chip the atom
into a little wedge to smash the world?
The mother crosses her fingers or her front
and bathes the little one in holy water
and castile soap. And all the morning stars
continue singing. And the infant grows.

Day by day she teaches him this thing:
to be vertical, to rear his belly up
from earth which seems to pull his navel string
still harder than she held it in the womb.
The earth cries: You are mine, you shall be mine
at last. Why trouble with the time between?

But the mother urges him to stand. And all his life
she counsels him to stand until a blow
harder than all the others takes his breath
and he lies quiet. And the count is ten.
This is the sovereign dignity of man,
she teaches him: ever to be erect
even if it is on the cross, until the flesh
is empty of the ghost, is simple dust.

She teaches him to use his hands. She prays his hands
are shaped for art, not murder. In the shop
he copies his father with the plane and chisel.

A chisel can be a weapon or a tool.
If the child hate his parents, and be hurt
in his small vanities, the stool or table
he fashions may become an enemy
magically murdered with the flying hammer,
and Christ is a criminal whose piteous doom
rests at his mother's or his father's door.

And if he be secure in love, then give him
bayonets for his carving tools, he'll make
cradles and roodscreens in a lace of wood.

But if he be reared with neither hate nor love
but only science and psychology,
then give him bayonets and call them tools
or chisels, calling them weapons. It's all the same.
Nourished past good and evil, what he'll make
will have no moral, being only power.

He is the priest of energy. His god is dust
triumphant in the heaven. Let us reject
this blasphemy before the final bomb
tries out the flesh, that vessel of our thought,
to simple chemistry, and at a blinding stroke
both cures our sin and cancels its redemption.

III

With such devoted eyes the saints of science
gaze into matter as the saints of God
stare at the spirit, narrowing the lids
to look for truth. The faithful parent answers
each single question of the seeking child
or blights him, and the spirit of the world
no more denies its suitor, but gives up
the treasure asked of it. No question is immoral,
but every answer carries life or death.

Perhaps the wish of the spermatozoa
is death, and life the progress to that target.
Ask them. We know now nothing is impossible,
not even conversation with a microbe.

And yet, to prove a thing desirable
is wiser than to prove it possible:
a wisdom alien to this factual time.

The child in the workshop has been given leave
to exercise his curiosity
even to the limit. The chisel is displaced
by a small eye for prying into little boxes
looking for hope. Naturally the child
delights in littleness that makes his measure
appear gigantic. All children love a peepshow.
The atom is the smallest puppet spinning
in the smallest slot machine. And children love
the tale of the genie in the tiny flask
who, once uncorked, is bigger than the world.

So be it. Let them have their fairy tales.
But when the fairy tale, blown up by Disney,
steps off the screen and takes on weight and volume,
and Donald Duck, the maniac, obeys
his impulse in a world of three dimensions,

the audience leaves the seats and, running not walking,
batters itself to death against the exits.

Too late for counsel now. The nursery
has hatched a Titan that could knock it cold.
The demon-ghost behind the devil mask
has made itself a body from our terror,
and death, that was our individual fate,
blackmails us as our universal doom,
while we reply at large: we do repent,
though of what we're not quite certain, nor to whom.

IV

This story has no moral. It is written at a time
when eyesight is too poor to read that word,
being perhaps befogged a little by a cloud
of smoke from Nagasaki. That town and Hiroshima
are somewhere now among the stars. Young children
blown into constellations, tiny worlds
too far and small for seeing; paper houses
puffed to the substance of a faint remorse.

Thrilling to see into how rare a dust
a town can flower, thinning out and out
until the border between thought and matter
is not discernible, whether to thought or lens.

And since the scientist is one who seems
always about to come to some conclusion,
we, who *are* about to come to some conclusion,
pose this hypothesis concerning science:

Science reveals fragility of matter
in contrast to the grossness of the mind,
the grandeur of the dusty universe
beside the smallness of the human heart.

V

Enough of bitterness. The ironic tongue
speaks for the stricken heart, but only half the truth.
And whether scientist or alchemist,
there was an arch-Initiate who drew
in dust a runic circle round the soul,
a circle called the womb. And I who am a woman
recall what ghost was summoned to that center
and how that ghost was love and is my son
and is the spirit and the flesh conjoined
and is mankind, who as he once was born
out of the body, can be born again
into the Holy Ghost, world without end.

Against the bomb there can be no defense
except the spirit. If our towns be rubble,
we'll take the stones and carve them into bison
and carp and reindeer and the leaping salmon,
and write upon them with sharp smaller stones
poems and epitaphs and epigrams
for the dead lovers, for the murdered children,
the old people and the pets, the toby jugs,
the football trophies and the legion buttons
and crucifixes, the whole way of life
that asked for death, and got it.

Remembering our mother's counsel to stand up
till we're knocked down, though God himself may seem
bent on destruction of his tired creation,
though we may dream we see an idiot hand
write "This is it" across a swaying wall,
we'll take some pride, however pitiful and futile,
in keeping upright while the stars fall down.

VI

The mind, that sees the clock-face as a circle,

disbelieves time's end. But clocks can stop.
The heart too is a clock. So is the sun.

Like science, poetry must fix its thought
in thing and symbol. Time is a shadow
cast on a Roman number cut in stone.
Love is a little boy whose flesh is flowers
or an ageing woman in an empty house.
Hate is a pedagogue grown sick of knowledge.
Annihilation is a planet blown
into its components: atoms, electrons.
The mind refuses emptiness, disbelieves death
and in infinity is lost and far from home.

This is a world and not a theorem.
This is the earth, not a magnetic object
attractive mainly to the scientists,
potential only for the powerful.
This is no penny for the ill-directed
to toss up at a crossroads. This is the earth,
my domicile, in whose domestic order
I have a voice, small but authoritative.

This is my father's and my mother's home.
Do it no harm. I love it. It is mine.
I charge you not for any frivolous reason
of curiosity or greed or fear
to scar it anywhere. Do not hurt one island,
no, not the littlest atoll, in the name
of science or security. I say:
This is my Father's house. Behave yourselves.

Go dig and build and write and paint and make
music and some mistakes and love and laws
and never seek again the philosophers' stone.
For who would seek a stone if he might eat,
by asking for it, of the living bread?

VII

Let science serve us. Let the scientist
be our best servant since he cannot be
our wisest master, since indeed no man
can be our master. The mind that would control
the atom must itself be ruled by love,
and love is union of all kindly men.

There is no secret locked away in matter
to make the future safe. There is no future
of equal wealth and self-sustaining peace.
There is no cure for war except the wish
wakeful forever in the present being.

For us there are only now and you and I,
the holy child, the star, and the small world.
This glance, this word, this touch, this understanding
flowing from each of us to every other
now and forever in simple charity
are the small rudiments of our salvation.

And all we are and do must be confined
within the instant. We cannot save the world
tomorrow or the next day or the next.
If we would save the world we'll have no chance
except this moment that passes as it comes.

Late 1945–early 1946

Men at Work

A Common Tree

There was a man
who climbed a tree
and hung there
for each man to see
what shape and size
a man should be.

1949 (?)

Twi-Horned Creature

Creation of beauty is the delight of man,
blasting of the beautiful is his delight.
The rose window is his craft, the bridge, the page of print,
and to kill the metal-feathered duck in panic flight.

The beast and his domain are narrow and pure.
The wolf has hunger, but has not cross nor rope.
The width from good to evil is man's range.
Earth is his fulcrum, hell or heaven his scope.

Weep for the wounded flesh but not for timely death,
and not for pain, but for its cruel cause.
Sever the gangrened hand from the conscious man,
but gently open the trap from the mink's bloody paws.

Fall, 1948

Except Ye Become . . .

With how intense a fire the celibate
purifies suffering until she gleams:
a bare knife pointed at the breast of life.

But savager than this, the married prude
wraps her necessities in muslin fibs
and hangs wax fruit on Eden's groaning tree,

while children, beasts, and lovers, lax and whole,
walk muddyfooted into Kingdom Come.

1948 (?)

The Uncreation

I made a man doll. From its side
another issued, this a girl
of bisque and flax, erotic bride.
They lay beneath a tree of pearl.

A serpent made of gems on wire
was coiled among the writhing root
and from the boughs, like eyes of fire,
hung down the blown glass of the fruit.

How should the angel now be kept
from coming?—Abel saved from death?
Over the dreamers while they slept
I stooped and drank away their breath.

1947 (?)

(Another form of this poem, "I Made a Man of Cretan Clay," is
printed on page 289. "The Uncreation" is probably the later version.)

Men at Work

Danger, danger, oh everywhere danger.
Nothing is safe. The burning stars explode.
The beautiful insect bears death, the bright snake, death.
Love is a vacuum. The eyes of mortals
are to each other dangerous wells of pain.
To be born is the great risk. Death only is no gamble.
A man should be afraid to blink his eye.
Like a scared mouse he might couch in grass, waiting
with famished look, for silence, to dart forth for food
and then return to wait with hope for death.

But man is praiseworthy. And very vile.
He goes forth walking on a rope of light,
not fearing to fall but seeking to murder angels.
He kisses poisoned water to salute his own loved lips.
He makes promises of metal and prisons of envy.
He has discovered love, dreamed Christ, paid Judas,
imagined freedom, pursued happiness, lost joy.

1947 (?)

The Old Men of Hate

I live in a house infested
by ancient, jealous men.
Some of them are dying. Some
are dead.
What is alike in all is that
they hate my sons.
The thoughtful, glad young men
and infant boys they hate.
And they will kill them, they
will find again, again the way
to kill them.

Early 1949

Norwich, Vermont, 1954

Seattle, Washington, October, 1935

Norwich, Vermont, c. 1957

The Unteachable

The grave is packed, as a bride's chest with linen,
with dead reasons for dying, heirlooms that the bride
finds new to her use.
                              That her mother's maidenhead
was plucked does not account for hers. Violence
of the bed needs to be done anew each time
and brutal battle is not printed in the son's
nerves from the father's wounds, but must be known
in the present flesh.
                              Children are unhistorical.
Cheat me not, the child says, of learning my own grief,
which is unique and not like yours. Alas!
Can nothing be taught or shown?
                              The grandsire sighs,
stretches his branchy hand to save the headlong children
who think the old man crazy and half dead.

1948 (?)

Paratroopers

Image of boys falling to doubtful futures,
drilled youth making fact of prophesy
that was its childhood's glee: the game of jumping.
Image of a sequence of frail domes
sunshading out to ease the unthinkable drop:
domes that are the careful breasts of battle,
nursing the young to the lonely mission, depositing them
gently on journeys to ungentle ends.

There is such tender forethought in these means:
that fewest bones may break, that most may survive
hell's taste, hate's dose. These caught lives are let down,
in one sense and another, with such science
that admiration stirs. There's such a valorous beauty
in the event, the evil of its cause
is for an instant, by a spring of tears,
distorted, made to shine.

February–April, 1949

The Signs

Poverty and love and thought
put their stigmata on the flesh.

The farmer squinting at the sun
until his face is all in pleats

looks like the suffering Christ who gazed
into the hot greeds of men.

The girl by the adobe house,
whose belly is big, whose cheekbones stare,

is the Madonna carrying
the universe within her womb.

The man who thinks for his fellow man
has the face of a tortured Jew.

1948 (?)

Maidanek, Dachau, Buchenwald

A Note for San Francisco

At first they made me ill. At first they made me wish to die. Or kill.
At first I wished to turn from them. To run. To hide.
I hated food, which being denied to them, became a measure of their
   death.
So horror grew in me. So illness. So they lay, loathly, forsaken.
So they were killed twice, once by their butchers, once by my guts'
   revulsion.

You know of whom I speak. You too have turned aside
shuddering. But the matter is too huge.

Horror is over, by its own too-muchness overborne.
Disgust is over. Only love remains.

Let me look at them a long long while with love.
I cannot touch their flesh. I cannot cradle their sleep.
I have only these pictures: silver aseptic shadows
of the red and mudded stinking screaming fact.

But I shall look at these a long long while with love:
these pictures of ditches filled with rows of famished Christs,
of male and female Christs and thin Christ children
carved by hunger to Gothic essential bone,
nailed by horror each to his lonely cross.

My God, my God, why hast thou forsaken them?

That the incorrigible might be corrected,
the powers rebuked, the world remade.

One Christ was not enough.

May, 1945

Nightmare

See where the families stand about in the estuary
on the polished water. The banker and his children
grin at one another with green smiles.

When the water opens its lips and swallows one of them
the others go on chatting. If anyone should
jitter and move to rescue, the water might
snap at him too. Do nothing. For a little
longer stand on the solid water. For a little
longer believe the water solid. Don't look down
or you'll see Henry at the bottom looking sick or dead,
tangled with a galleon or a submarine.

October, 1946

Ballad of the Young Dog Fox

There was a young dog fox
and a gay young dog was he.
He cocked an eye at a white chicken
all in the south countree.

 With a rang and a tang and a pluck pluck

And all the hunting gentlemen
in that sweet countryside
they whistled their hounds and got their guns.
"It's time that dog fox died."

 With a ring and a ting and a long long run

They didn't need to breach a keg
for they were drunk without.
They rode through swamp, they rode through grass.
They knew what they were about.

 With a pluck and a twang and a high high swing

But oh the smart old game warden
had caught the young dog fox.
He'd locked him up in a good safe pen
with a couple of big Yale locks.

 With a hey and a ho and a thin hope

And all those gentle gentlemen
were wild as wild can be.
Who dares to cheat us of our chase
all over the south countree?

 With a rang and a tang and a black black

They tied the warden up in a chair.
They broke the big Yale locks.
With a roar and a rush and a peal of hounds
they chased that young dog fox.

    With a curse and a blow and a whip whip

They caught that fox in the middle of a wood
they got him in a ring
as plain to shoot as a big bullseye
but they did no such thing.

    With a laugh and a wink and a hey what sport

They roped his feet and they cut his balls
they whipped his shuddering hide
then hung him high on a live-oak limb
and ripped him up his side.

    With a rang and a tang and a great good time

And home they rode to breakfast
and home they rode to their wives,
a pretty pack of gentlemen
who'd had the time of their lives.

    With a grin and a shrug and a white Christ mass.

Spring, 1947

All Lovers

Save for the wholly personal longing of two beings
for each other's presence and possession
what is the taproot of the social tree?
Except that Robert lay with Ruth and got her with child
the Senator would not now harangue the Senate
to pass a bill to benefit a nation
hatched in the loins of lovers who thought only
to lose themselves in gaining one another.

Beware when people are perceived as categories
and not as names or souls. Phyllis and Eric,
Joel and Rebeccah, Sven and Garda; speak their names
with your living breath and do not call them masses
races or classes, since the abstract lie
de-faces their humanity, gelds their sex,
who are all lovers and children of desire.

Fall, 1945

Hemisphere

The leaf-sail bends to a boy's breath.
The chip-boat runs on the ribbed water.
The dreams of Wren roar down in crumbs of stone.
Here only apples cannonade the grass.

Blow, boy! God growls around the sky
in Autumn thunder. What if the curdling snarls
of the Prime Minister disrupt the ether?
They do not pass your eardrums.

But when the first black raindrops pit the pool,
look up. See the angry cloud. You are afraid,
not of God, not of death; of loneliness only.
Run home.

October, 1940—September, 1941

Homo Winesap

Man, to assert his dignity,
abstracts himself from history.

The apple has no memory.
Existing in a wooden box
it does not know there was a tree.

And so you see there was no tree.
The apple is entirely free.

Early 1949

The Great Alien

The crashed aviatrix and the startled lion
met. Loved curiously. Joined on the blond sand.

Rescued, returned to her city, the woman wept,
amputated of her peerless mate.

When she gave birth the child had tawny hair
on all his height. No tail. But a thick mane
and vigilant eyes that peered as though through bars.

He grew a comely man with great voice
used seldom except in nightmare, when he roared.

He paced the alien city, grew great with scorn.

He mined the savage city and destroyed it,
even his mother. Fled to the broad sand

to find his father, a beast magnificent,
wordless and dangerous. He slew him. Roared his grief
and stalked through night and day

and found no mate.

Fall, 1945

Lethal Tool

Channel of meaning, nothing understanding, the ear serves life and
    death.
So do the eye, the hand, the genitals.
But quickest of all, most terrible: the tongue.

Warm obscene moist busy muscle, the tool of spite,
loose in a head it can wreck towns, poison wells.

Hideous toad, pink dwarf, it squats in its mucous cave
rooted to brain and stomach. It has two works:
to pulp figs, lettuces, grains, birds, the bodies of lambs
and to wig-wag what's in the mind.

Think clear and it speaks clean. Think foul or small,
it drools an epidemic on the map:

hatred bitterness divorce mistrust madness fury everlasting war.

Spring, 1944

Big Toy

War has no eyes, it has no mind.
It winds up with a key behind.

It goes the way its clockwork leads,
committing memorable deeds.

And when its spring is all unwound,
it whirs, and crashes on the ground.

Then gadget-minded children find it.
They tinker it together, wind it

and set it on its gadget feet.
The clockwork stirs. Repeat—repeat.

1949

Previously
Uncollected
Poems

1921-1951

Walking

I walked on a snow-bank that squeaked like leather,
Or two wooden spoons that you rub together;

I walked on green moss and brown earth, sprouting
With little grass blades on their first spring outing.

I walked on blossoms and cool, green cresses,
And grass that rustled like silken dresses;

I walked on bracken, and dry leaves after,
That flamed with color and crackled with laughter.

.   .   .

I walked on the earth as the seasons came,
And under my feet it was never the same!

1921

Little Brothers

In the brightflowering fields
by man's hand tilled,
cropped by the teeth of beasts,
and older than beast or man,—
in the newflowering fields
the new lambs gambol,—
the lambs, ambassadors of love
from the sheep's dumb hearts
to the blind minds of men.

And the children, ambassadors of pity
from men's dulled hearts
to the beseeching sheep,
seeing the lambs in the flowers,
cry out for joy, and with their love
win pardon for their predatory sires
from the bereaved earth mother
for the spilled blood of her beasts.

1920's (?)

The Beautiful Lady without Choice

In a dream green with leaf-light,
in sunshot gloom of woods,
by birds attended,
and by furred, unfearing beasts,
she moves in mercy, she moves in music,
and her hair is writhen copper
and larkspur blue her gown.

Pitiful Mary, sister of grace and peace,
pause and ponder, be prepared for pain.
Hide the affrighted pheasants,
for the wind
is loud and bitter with the speech of guns.
Hide them in crypts of bracken
brown and deep
lest men take and hang them like dappled fruit
by their killed claws.

Sorrow, sorrow.
Frost is a silver sword.
The blazing panes have fallen
from the arboreal mullions
and pity turns murderess at the whip of need.
Through birdless woods she treads a fungoid floor
and shivers in a cloak of squirrel skins.
And her eyes are drained,
are drained even of grief.
And her hair is bitter white.

1927

Old Houses

These old frame houses
grey and dim as dusk,
all winter long have stood
like quiet doves
through wet, grey days.

Now cold March sunshine
touches them to life,
and lemon-bright they gleam
among wet branches
of black and leafless trees.

There are no pigments
delicate enough
to put their shadows
and frail, faded colours
onto flat paper.
All their ugliness
of paintless surface
and unclassic shape
is lost in lemon light
and dove grey shadow,
so that they shimmer
in the rain-wet air
like domiciles of dream.

I think of stucco houses
screaming white,
carved with strong shadows
by a cruel sun.
I think of flaming roofs
of scarlet tile,
and blue glazed jars
with shoulders flashing light

standing in oval arches,
and small trees
shining with oranges.

I think of those and these,—
those laughing colours
under the South's bright sun,—
this Northern silver,—
that positive beauty
and this subtle magic
of hideous houses
made so beautiful
by the swift ruin
of the rainy years.

1928

Time . . . and Springtime

A choir of birds enticed me away
From the dull routine of an ordinary day,
From the man-made tasks and the self-made sorrows,
Remorse for the yesterdays, fears for the morrows,
From the pulse of a clock in a lonely room,
Shuttling the minutes on the day's large loom,
From the thrall of books, with their shapes of thought
Sepulchered in words, like flowers once brought
From a bee-lulled field and the sun-sweet air
And pressed to the shells of the things they were.

And I walked in the ways where the birds were thick
As buds on the trees, and my blood was quick
With the sweet of the world in the singing of the day,
And my feet were light with their own rondelay.
Oh, the songs bewitched of the birds' small tongues!
Oh, the clean, warm air in winter-weathered lungs!

I put my ear to a tree's hard trunk,
And the tree was alive, and crazy . . . and drunk
With the wine of the world in its old, old veins,
With the passion of the sun and the quick spring rains.
And its green tongues spoke where the wind moved through:
"Behold!—I am alive again!—What, then, of you? . . .
I, who was dead, shake blossoms to the sun,—
Life, that dies forever, is never, never done!"

And there by the tree with bloom of scented snow,
I knew that beauty passes as seasons come and go,
That loveliness is born again as seasons go and come,
That every day is one day, since many make a sum,—

That every year is one year . . . and then, of course, I knew
That time is a fable that is only half true.

1928

Quatrain

I know not why I am,
But, with the world about me,
I am content that earth
Was not content without me.

Romance

"A gel must not be serious. It's alahming
when pretty gels do other than be chahming."
So spake Lord Harry of the Nth Hussars,
squeezing my hand and sighing at the stars.

Silent, I thought how Harry'd find it shocking
if he should learn the color of my stocking
or spy a brain beneath my cap and bells
far from the calibre prescribed for gels.

I thought: I must be careful, and should Harry
propose it, I must not consent to marry.
Woe to the happy British upper classes
when wives make husbands look like silly asses.

Since Harry hunts the Fox and I the Muse,
I'd like to post him with some cheerful news:
When gels grow older and a shade less pretty,
a little intellect is no great pity.

1930 (?)

Anthropoeides

In the brain of the dumb brute
dig and find the mandrake root.

Lore as old as life I cull
from the flat and narrow skull.

Through the speaking eyes I reach
meaning bodied not in speech.

Hungers never such as mine
plead their cause in wag and whine,

yet those needs are gnomish embers
of a state my blood remembers.

Brother dog, beneath the skin
you and I are close akin,

cousined in the shallow head
of a brute millenniums dead

that upon his witless she
drew the diagram of me.

Mandrake root and mental seed
in the brutish body breed;

faith that I have left behind
governs still the wordless mind:

God, believe it if you can,
has the contour of a man.

Early 1930's

Shopping List

One ouakari
two toucans
three thrips
four foraminifera
five filefish
six silkworms
seven setters
eight eiderducks
nine nightcrawlers
ten tent caterpillars
eleven elephants
twelve twigborers
thirteen thistlecocks
fourteen foraging ants
fifteen finches
sixteen sickelbills
seventeen secretary birds
eighteen eyras
nineteen nightingales
twenty twitlarks

Charge them please

Early 1930's

To the Importunate One

Sometimes it's grief I feel—more often, fury
That you should move my heart to these extremes
Of cold dislike. Your love too much presumes
Upon a patience that has long grown weary.
You are a gardener in so great a hurry
To force your flowers from their natural stems
That bloom goes by before true summer comes
And mirth is over that should still be merry.

Why stroke the cat till surfeited with stroking
She thinks it heaven to be left alone?
Leave me in peace. You lose me with your seeking.
If you had loved me well you would have seen
How for that loving I have little liking
Which strives to bind me to its own design.

1933

Violin

I see the spatulate fingers
touching the tenuous gut,
awaking joys and angers
in the fiddle's dark throat.

Wood made thin as a leaf
and colored to dark amber
holds rapture, holds grief
within its curving chamber.

1933

Intimate Apocalypse

I will pull the sky more close,
I will spin a tight cocoon
with a little private sun
and a little secret moon.

In those confines closely curled,
from my own galactic fire
I shall forge another world
in the shape of my desire.

None shall strut in crown or robe,
whip or sabre none shall bear.
These shall populate the globe:
Bach and Pierrot and Voltaire.

1937 (?)

The Latest Puritan

A latter exile to this pilgrims' place,
I find it consonant with something old
before my time, as if the ties of race
proffered me privilege and gave me hold
upon the land. Already I am bound
more closely, with more chance of flower and fruit,
than since I was uptorn from Dorset ground
to grow amiss, being stricken at the root.

They called the land New England, they who came
from that old England of our common birth.
And I have followed them to take the same
urgent possession of an alien earth,
to drive as they did into healing loam
a torn stalk destined to a second home.

1937 (?)

New England

The Wish of the Immigrant

Blue, undulant, like waves held still in time,
against a cliff of sky the far hills climb.
Tawny, like lions coated close with gold,
the fields lie shorn to April. Quick and cold,
the brooks, long bottled in pale celadon,
crackle their glaze and break the mold and run
past naked elms, by birches white as bone,
and maple roots, and walls of meadow-stone.
Like diagrams of branching veins and nerves
the bare trees trace the sky. The earth preserves
tatters of snow in hollows, under pines
where needles will be cool when August shines.
In quiet masses, sensitively planned
to fit the curving body of the land,
rest buckling houses in huge nests of faded
silos and barns, by time and lack invaded.
I wish for such a house among these hills,
with beauty flowing in across its sills,
a house to catch against its windows' glass
the snow, the sun, the seasons as they pass,
to fade when I have faded, yet be there
printed forever, ghostly, on the air.

1937 (P)

Bird of Easter

*In mediaeval Christian symbolism the
pelican turns matricide on Good Friday. On Easter morning she pecks her
breast and revives her children with a
baptism of her blood.*

Miserere! Christ interred.
Cursed the tree whereon he hung.
Silence has engulfed the Word
and the hieroglyphic bird
slays her young.

Fabulous infanticide!
Passion of the pelican!
Pierced for love her children died.
Christ the Lord is crucified,
pierced for man.

Let the lily split the cell.
Let the tomb be dispossessed.
Christ three days has walked in Hell.
Pelican, the legends tell,
tears her breast.

Blood whose potence love has priced,
rain of ruby bearing breath,
resurrects the sacrificed.
Jubilate! Cry that Christ
conquers death.

March 30, 1940

Aim

Guncrack
and fall of feathers
to indifferent earth.
Guncrack
and acrid breath
on autumn air, a
blue wreath crawling
from thin metal mouth.
Guncrack.
The wounded bird
to bracken stricken
the heart split
and the clean quills
broken.
Guncrack.
Sportsman
lower your gun.
You are the mark.
Guncrack.

April 14, 1940

Let Me Hold You Far

We miss each other when we are too near.
When we are far we see each other clear.

Early 1940's (?)

Now the Instructed Mind

Earth was a declaration,
the sun a thought,
the sky
a precept to the recording senses.

Now the instructed mind
looks to an inward landscape
rather than through
pupil and casement
to the memorized meadow.

1941 (?)

Assignment

I have not touched this horror,—known the smell
of ruin and torture, nor have heard their sound.
But the grey newsprint halftone reeks of hell
enough for fury. Bodies broken and drowned,
and cities leveled, stamped in black and white,
harry the conscience and obscure the sight.

The fault was mine. But while the arches crack
of custom and the insufficient norm,
I rear my son to labor and to lack,
I bless my son with sinew for the storm.
Ride it, my son!—With all its rage beneath you
make justice of the havoc I bequeath you.

March 18, 1941

Drink-Me

Learn to see and to say in the world's way. Then we'll
say: Un-see, un-be as the world. See again as a child.
Reject the fact. Go back to the act, the spring, the
will, the thought, not the thing. Don't be caught in
the ring of the wrong, but be taught by the young and the mad to be
    glad and be strong.

To be uncurst of your sin, try on first the skin of
Rousseau's lion. Do so, then wake for truth's sake
Blake's tiger to roar truth bigger, error smaller, and
scare thought's squalor.

Contrive to engrave bison on mammoth tusk. Hasten through
dusk to read a reminder of reindeer rubbed in a cave. Then,
be brave! Write a line like Stein.

Draw a picture like Picasso or baby: an arm with a fracture,
or maybe two heads to one torso. Warp a man to a harp,
like Arp, only more so. Paint a quaint train in a bed of
flowers, or a green sun in a red rain-shower.

So gain an innocent power. Break fake. Bring the ego in
butterfly wings from the black. Crack the chrysalis.
Loose the imago. Be free. Un-see and un-be.

Summer, 1941

Black-out

The flippered mole
With his frilled snout
Furrows and burrows
His way about.

With feet like fins
He swims in loam
And with his whiskers
Lights his home.

July, 1941

Easter Egg Cracked

Crocus waker
Cock of Spring
break your brittle
sky and sing!

Crowing Sun
cry death undone.

Early 1940's (?)

Druid

At twelve years old I worshipped trees.
Their bodies, with their wrinkled skins,
gave my spirit strength and ease
and shrived me of my childish sins.

Wherever seed of tree had built
its candled altar on the air
I dropped such load of grief and guilt
as twelve years old has learned to bear.

With little science and much sense
I thought a tree a lightening rod
that dealt to earth at heaven's expense
the bright electric shock of God.

Early 1940's (?)

Nursery Rhyme

When the small foetus
hung like a fruit,
its fingers leaves
its navelstring root,
I was the sky
I was the earth
I was the axle
of being and birth.

Then the small foetus
was born and he cried
and he was the center
of wonder and pride.
He was the center
and him I must enter
and always wrapped up in him
now I must ride.

Early 1940's

Private Entry in the Diary of a Female Parent

He is my own fault. Let me see it straight.
I got him willfully, with joy, and hatched him
a long time intimately, and in him warmed
the flaws and fineness of two ancestries,
before I had my bellyful of him
at last and threw him neck and crop
into the doctor's expert rubber hands.
Since then I've suckled, kissed and smacked him
while he has sucked and wet and beaten me
or all but beaten me, although I rise
out of the ashes at short intervals.
The end will be, perhaps, the end of me,
which will, I humbly guess, be his beginning.

Early 1940's

A Matter of Fact

FOR LOUIS UNTERMEYER

"What do you know about the Tamarack?"
You asked the question apropos of nothing.
"The Tamarack," I answered, "sheds its needles
although it poses as an evergreen."
You seemed so pleased by such a simple answer,
I asked you why. You said: "That is a fact
solid and bright to cling to when the world
breaks in your fingers. That, or any fact,
is something certain for the mind to clutch
and cling to through disaster." When my walls
shatter about me, I shall think of you
thinking of facts as though they were salvation,
and of the Tamarack that drops its leaves.

August, 1942

The Great Doors

The spirit in his prison groans:
a living angel walled with stones.

And—Let me out! the angel cries,
battering lightward through the eyes.

But all the freedom he can win
through five strait doors is smuggled in.

Shape and sound, stuff, flavor, smell,
turn keys into his private hell

till, six and seven, are pushed apart
the great doors of the mind and heart.

November, 1942

Provident Season

The small obscene and necessary worm
divides our cubits by its agile fraction
and stirs us in our sleep. The dead are common
as dirt, an equal people, wardens of power.
Out of the negative, out of canceled color
shall come the nubile flower. November is no dolor
denying June. A conservative spirit moves
intent upon a profound housekeeping.

Early 1940's (?)

Mirror Thought

Roots branch through earth's enclosing night.
Branches are rooted to the light.
What if the worm sees by a spark
That makes him pity the bird's dark?

1943 (?)

Conversation between the Curies

PIERRE:

You may break light and see its component parts
in a ladder of color along a wall. You break it through a prism.
Through what shall we pass ourselves that we may do
as Socrates told us?—to know ourselves, to see
our spectrum? the separate colors of our ghost?

MARIE:

Work is a prism, Pierre. It is work that breaks us
and shows us what we are. I'd like to think
that when I'm dead the ghost of what I did
will glow a little longer on the air
in an analysis of what I was.

1943 (?)

Quest of Truth

The molecule is hard to climb.
I cannot scale the sides of time.

Knowledge is a pulse of light
under a hill of hematite.

I thrust my thought in the cold rock
and die before I budge the lock.

1943 (?)

Timber Crew

Timber! I remember the cry,
the new and lonely warning of small man
pricking the antique morning.

Among the verticals of pine
suddenly a leaning line.

Not a king—a kingdom—a city of fiber falls
with groaning walls.

Stand. Let squirrels do the running
from ruin tilted by your cunning.

Tree's calculated green trajectory
saves you from retribution.
A century's load
thuds. The hills applaud
precisely, without passion,
your minute's victory.

Early 1943

Funeral of Clocks

There is no peace. The righteous clock
who utters minutes in my head
admonishing with nick and knock
my slow resemblance to the dead
is like a cricket in a can,
is like an ant upon the skin.
There is no hope for me and man
to shrive us of our earthly sin.

There would be hope if there were time,
there would be time if calendars
and clocks were shriven of their crime
on pyres beneath the leisured stars,
leaving the planet's quiet wheel
to brake the hurry of our heel.

Early 1943

Second Expulsion

I love you with a love that's set
over you like an airless tent.
My love confines you, as a net,
and binds you, as a sacrament.
If you would tower to a man
and be what I would have you be,
fear me and flee me when you can—
be curt, be cruel, but be free.

I am the strength to be withstood.
I am the kindness not to trust.
I may not keep you though I would.
I would not lose you, and I must.
This let me learn, so hear me warn:
woman's son must twice be born.

March 14, 1943

Dimensional Rhyme

Space is a box whose walls are time.
How long it takes a thought to climb
bottom to cover, side to side,
measures how high it is and wide.

1943

The Smile

I smiled at an old man who, with a resigned despair
resembling contentment, swept the street.

My smile fell into his surprised, weak eyes
and made the circuit of his antique bones.

Therein it must have found strong residue of joy,
for it returned to me much fortified.

1944 (?)

The Answer

To the question posted in the eyes of children the
    answer is:
conquest, devastation, the armies of corruption
    marching in slovenly triumph.

The walls open like books. We read burst arteries
of water systems, wallpaper shouting
patches whence pictures have fallen in a gasp of glass.

This is the civilized bargain, the lesson bought and sold.
This is the right total to the wrong calculation.
This is the answer at the end of the obsolete text book.

But a few of the children, crying their contempt,
push their teachers aside, and arise and stand on their desks
and grasp their chalk and write across black heaven
blazing equations of the zodiac.

1944

Who Is Not Who

God is not Who.
He, being one and three,
dissolves the person,
breaks the walls of who.

God is not Why.
Certainly, I
deem him not a question
but a reply.

God is not When.
The artifice called Time
is an acrostic rhyme
of sensual use to men.

God is not Where.
Seek and ye shall not find
pity or love or mind
in earth, fire, water, air.

If God be What,
certainly I have not
found man of God to prove
what God is or is not.

God being naught
that any man has thought,
of what God is
the certainty is his.

Early 1944

Occult Adventure

Through every surface of my skin
the needles of the pines struck in.

The blind trees through my pupils could
see themselves: a winter wood.

With the shared organ of my ear
when the bird cried, the bough could hear.

Sucked dry by every staring bud,
identity forsook my blood.

I was the wood's uprooted ghost,
the self, half guessed, of that cold host.

Snow fell to snow. I woke. My skis
shot with my self beyond the trees.

April–May, 1944

In a Dry Season

Man displayed on the cross of your own corpse,
knock out the nails, get down and walk.
The self is fossil wood, vertical and horizontal.
Isn't it enough that you have dragged it slowly
all the days of your life to the public hilltop?
Must you also hang there till the kites dive?
Get down and live, adorned with your five wounds.

June 3–4, 1944

Great and Small

I lost the world, the magical
blueweathered world of smell and sound
by growing up to five foot six.
At this sane distance from the ground
the child's dominions shrivel small,
his rafts are doormats and his guns are sticks.

And yet a child, not I, but mine,
continues in that world of sense
and makebelieve, to breathe and dream.
My past is in his present tense.
I know, but cannot cross, that line
near which he watches what I am, or seem.

O questioner with candid eyes
held wide to drink all wonder deep
till disenchantment drowns their blue!
You long to buy (and think it cheap)
stature with innocence. But size
increased, can dwindle what you are, and do.

Late 1944

Pinwheel

I fear one minute more than twenty years.
In twenty years, my darling, you and I
may grow to fit our futures. We may die
or part, or learn forbearance. Today's fears
cause me to clap my hands against my ears.
This coming moment screeches from our sky
harsh as a bomb. Flung on my face I lie
tense, till the rowdy rumor of it clears.

The past is peace and quiet, or at most
dreams in a sleep. Far future is a risk
not yet to take. All time's a harmless ghost
except this minute, pressing harsh and brisk
onto the next, spun like a croupier's disk
with all our kindness to be won or lost.

Middle 1940's (?)

Bone Has a Ghost

Bone has a ghost whose name is flesh
and flesh a ghost whose name is thought
and thought a ghost whose name is God
and He what ghost we are not taught.

        Yes, the Holy Ghost.

Middle 1940's (?)

Eros in a Graveyard

The blind roots clutch the haunted mold.
Black boughs weep yellow leaves.
The wind along the churchyard grieves
and I am shaking cold.

Your mouth is like a good small fire
that warms me with its flame.
The dead would wake had they the same
to kindle their desire.

They lie now in a loveless bed
who living lay like this.
Keep from my hearing with your kiss
the choked sighs of the dead.

Middle 1940's (?)

Epitaph

Here lies a woman by hiatus killed.
She did no deed except what others willed.
She knew no grief, had no sins to forgive,
in suffering death guessed briefly how to live.

Middle 1940's (?)

Fish

Fish
hang in the crystal tank.

Fin-fanned, they balance
on bannisters of water.

What firm and fairy hand
could snaffle their small jaws?

Through gills of gold
they breathe the moted water.

The cameras of their eyes,
candid and comprehensive,
drink light, unwinking.

See in tank-like cases of museums
sweetness of Sung plates,
moon-green, smooth as snail;
Ming vases or lily cups of jade,
wherein have hands
petrified flying thought,
pinned transience to stillness.

The idea, fish, is coded being—
but here are immediate fish,
like colored Greek tear-glasses
set to music;
ephemeral selves, in coded messages—
calligraphy, quickened and lit,
from a Chinese brush—
a sacred dragon's wish
told in gold telegraphy.

Middle 1940's

How Music's Made

Study this violent and trembling woman
who is a gut strung from a star to a star
and when she's struck must twang till all the cups
and saucers ring and shake upon their shelves.
Forehear the note. Be thoughtful where you pluck.
How music's made is not a thing of luck.

Middle 1940's

Warning

Oh my dear, take care, take care!
There's dreadful danger everywhere.
Do not go near Orion or the Bear.
  They're all aflame!

Do not touch the earth. It turns.
Keep away from love. It burns.
There are snakes beneath the ferns
  no sorcerer can tame.

What's fair above is foul beneath.
Lie still, my darling. Hold your breath.
  Nothing is safe but death.

What! You are not afraid to die?
Then try the earth and risk the sky.

Middle 1940's

Landlocked

These waves which have risen
and do not fall
these hills that are my prison
this deaf wall
this tide of trance
this cataleptic ocean
shall gently lull me
with a lack of motion.

The blond grass shivers
under the wind's hand.
I bend my ear to the rivers
of this land.
I watch the kingbird
chase the hawk from heaven.
The temper of these fields
is still too even.

Here's a fair future:
peace for her who'll settle.
But mine's a nature
geared for a battle.
Restore me to those hills
that are salt to the lip,
can toss gulls at the sun
and wreck a ship.

Middle 1940's

To a Man Child

When you are grown
and work alone
high heart, clear brain,
clean ghost and bone,

look back to now.
Remember how
you, colt, were broken
to our plough.

Though wise, though fond,
this love's a bond
a man must wear
and walk beyond,

must seek, may find,
past bit and blind,
free love of kind,
free heart and mind.

Middle 1940's

Incorrupt

Before my father's bridges sprang in steel
or his pure chimneys climbed like reeds of stone,
their forms were fixed, their tensions were all known.
Then came the atomic function to reveal

in transient congress the immortal fact
pondered, in faith and quiet, by the mind.
Should war explode these yesses, one might find
blueprinted, negative, their truth intact.

Middle 1940's

In the Composed World

Here in the composed world how loud we wrangle,
our little mouths all crooked with their rage.
In our neat gardens tagged with pretty names
what flower do we sow more thick than acrimony?

Rude children with their eyes of stubborn truth
and shamefast dogs that vomit on the stair
are better mannered than the whipping man
who punishes their failure with his hate.

Middle 1940's

Lullaby

Sleep, my little one,
peacefully sleep.
Angels are near you
to guard and to keep.
Mother and Daddy
are proud of their son,
and when you are bigger
we'll buy you a gun.

Sleep, my pretty one,
gather your strength.
God and your country
will need you at length.
Dream on my bosom,
soothed by my touch,
and when you're a soldier
we'll buy you a crutch.

Middle 1940's

Function of the Historian

The cart tracks in the grass are hieroglyphic,
legend of one gone past into his future.
His load was heavy. See how flat the field,
scored like silver where the wheels have rolled.
The cart of wood has gone, but in its wake
has sown a furrow of its phantom selves
spun out in a parade of separate instants.
Review how at that hole one wheel went down
jolting the carter, making the cart oblique,
how there the big horse swerved to nip a pine,
and there he lagged a little at a mound,
making his master shake the bit and shout.
You've built the memory. Now fix it down
on rock or wax or paper for a relic
before the grass forgets the tracks in snow.

The picture's not exact. But it seems right.
The fact is finished. Let the fable grow.

Middle 1940's

Wisdom of the Body

All that the one may ask
or the other answer
fastens a tight mask
over the true person.

He speaks to a deaf ear,
he looks with a blind eye,
so each continues dear
to the imagined other.

Only the fingertips
know the simple truth,
only the lips,
the annealed, anonymous flesh.

Middle 1940's

The Bell

I from the belltower pour
bellsongs on the hour.

What if only children hear the tones
or only pigeons get it in their bones

not understanding it, or mice in the wall
feel it as simple thunderfall?

Even so, it is the bronze's own
voice, still metal tonguing tone,

still matter doing all it can,
even now the only thing it can,

hung there swinging over the town,
strung there unable to get down.

> I hang
> swing
> hang
> swing
> hang
> swing

1945 (?)

Morning Grouch

I think I shall not get to heaven.
But I hear news of it each day
from one who has not left it yet.

Time to get up   get up   get up!
Lazy Mummy will you get up!

O wicked child to be so young,
to run halfway to meet the morning!

1945 (?)

Trial by Fury

Shred the flesh
until the bones are clean:
Shake the tree
until the boughs are seen.

Fire your house
until the timbers glow.
You had not known its pattern.
Now you know.

Early 1945

Root and Branch

My feet, abused in all their bones,
ache among the leaves and stones.

Hard in November's rotting mesh
I stand to root my leafy flesh.

O melancholy ease of feet
surprised at finding it so sweet

to stand established cold and damp
in death's disintegration camp

while spouting sunward, partly free,
the fount of boughs, the human tree.

1945

Now as Ever

And still the earth turns,
beautiful wheel bearing horror,
through space of crystal
and diffracted blue.

And have the leaves not heard
that man intends his own destruction
that they cluster at roots
to make another spring?

What is the meaning of slaty pigeons
lifting through cold light
from rosered churchroof tiles?

To what purpose does the cream stone spire
thrust like a single spoke
to touch some armillary rim?

Why do our children's voices
still wound the heart
ringing through windows from schoolyards
in diamond mornings of November?

Does the squirrel not guess
the waste of his storage,
his thrift's futility?

Why do hammers drum building
while workmen curse, laugh, sweat
at their contract for ignoring doom?

Why does the fresh sweet lumber
smell as ever it did
of newbaked bread?

Why does the pulse applaud
even now the loft of cloud
and lateral light on fields of ivory stubble?

And should we sit at the recital,
stiff as Egyptian cats,
hearing Prokofieff speak from the struck keys
to make us maenads within?

O irresponsible joy! Pleasure bought on margin
by speculators who have lit already
the fuse beneath the bank.

But the pigeons and children have not seen
and could not understand the fuse
which anyway was always there and always lighted.

Nor can the heart, nor can the eye and ear
to which immortal death is intimate and alien.

November, 1945

Love Has So Terrible a Face

Love has so terrible a face,
a presence so beset with fear,
how may I bear his furious grace
or how endure and he not here?

He wrings my nerves with his sweet hands
and tears my wish as on a rack.
Eden is torment where he stands.
No ease is in his lack.

With cease of life the war may cease.
In brain and nerve is travail bred.
O peace on earth! There is no peace
save for the heartless and the dead.

1946 (?)

Search

I looked for God
on a Monday morning
among the rocks.
He was not there.

I looked for God
on a Tuesday morning.
I carefully rummaged
the upper air.

I looked for God
on a Wednesday morning
on the bed of the sea.
I found a crab.

On Thursday I sought him
in the city.
I found a man
in a chequered cab.

I looked for God
on a Friday morning
and found a priest
in a bombed-out chapel,

on Saturday sought him
in an orchard
and found a grub
in a windfall apple.

I looked for God
on a Sunday morning.
I found his name
in the Sunday book.

In fifty-two weeks
times forty years
there are still some places
where I might look.

1946

The Prophet

FOR MAX LERNER

I beat on doors of brass.
Open! Let me pass!

On windows as I travel
I rattle gravel.

I ring the still bells
till the sky swells.

I beat on bronze gongs
black news of wrongs.

Louder I roll my drums
warning you: God comes.

You smile. You think I rave. You
bind me. I tried to save you.

1946

Bearing Gifts

O six-year apparition, node of nerve,
green emanation of our limbs and dreams,
looking at us with eyes of ours, with eyes
that see we see you, with eyes we made to see.
You hear us with ingenious percussive
machines we wrought, the membranes and the channels
opening into the marvellous clustered brain.
How clever we were, not being clever at all
but only hungry and humble, mouth to mouth
and limbs knotted, passing the breath and seed
of life from one to other. Men are most skilled
forgetting skill, remembering only need,
only desire, only delight to make.

Give and ye shall receive—not ask, but give.
We gave ourselves each other and got you.
Stem, flower, fruit, you turn back to the tree
and ask the meaning and the origin.
And what is god or how the world began
we cannot answer save in children's tales
that even you can doubt. We do but feel
rain in our roots and you upon our boughs
and know ourselves a tree in a dark wood
wakened in spring by loud wings from the south.

1946

Dig No Hole

Dig no hole, my dear.
Neither hurry nor hide.
There is no furrow turned so deep
That death is left outside.

1946

Assignment

The maidens at Miss Walpole's School
transfixed me with their trustful eyes.
"What shall we do that we may taste
on earth the fruit of Paradise?"

"Do justice to your charms, my dears.
Lie with your lovers and conceive
children like cherubs. Nothing but love
is worth your trouble to believe."

But what I spoke was not the thought
they taught me with their petalled looks.
I said: "Read Auden. Cultivate,
my dears, a taste for the best books."

Spring, 1946

Cradle Cure

Whatever I have grown of fault
out of the seedy human land,
I bury in the basic sand,
cure in the fundamental salt.

From corn that bends me to the loam
before I break it from the stalk
I come down to the sea. I walk
back to my backbone's coral home.

Summer, 1946

Poem

The still air of September, the leaf lozenges falling in a spaced descent, diapering the air with tearshaped bombs of gold. They make a soft concussion with the fallen leaves and sound like footsteps bringing the frightened heart peace and release from the fear of death. For death at this moment is seen as coexistent with life and equal with it in value to the creation. There is sorrow in this falling and with it realization that sorrow is an experience as much to be desired as joy. There is melancholy in all returns, and this is the return of life to the dark earth, the spokes that have risen to their zenith coming down again, the season entering the small gate, the black tunnel of the seed from which it will sprout, ignorant of the death it has endured.

September, 1946

Temperature

Spring's fever soars
to Summer's height.
Up goes the green
mercurial thread.
But note, Nurse,
how in half a night
quicksilver falls
and Summer's dead.

October, 1946

Weigh, Hey!

Penny in the slot.
Learn your weight.
Take your ticket
and read your fate.

Bad tempered woman
milk gone sour
tarnished silver
wasted hour
C sharp flatted
racehorse lamed
bull's-eye blundered
proud man shamed
frost in summer
December thaw
flooded carburetor
toothless jaw
rainy holiday
faithless wife
train off schedule
edge off knife.

Hide the indicator.
Keep the news quiet.
Tear the ticket
and go on a diet.

October, 1946

The Natural-born

See how the sweet, sold acres
reflect the journey sun.
Gone to new caretakers,
farmer—your farm is done.

Here, where you bent your spine
to teach your fields to thrive,
the brash, the superfine,
the city folks arrive.

The view, we say, is worth
the price to buy your hills.
Into your father's earth
we thrust artesian drills.

But though we bore your bone,
harrow your nerves and mind,
this land, your flesh being sown,
will not give back your kind.

1947 (?)

Welcome Song

Farewell is forever.
When you come back
you'll find a stranger
answering your knock.
She will look like me
but look into her eyes.
See there the queer ghost
of your absent days.
Farewell is forever.
When you come home
I'll kiss a stranger
but he'll be welcome.

1947 (P)

I Made a Man of Cretan Clay

I made a man of Cretan clay.
He could not shout or breathe or sing.
He lay there on his side all day.
He did not think of anything.

I put red cloths around that mud.
And after years had passed, I found
on the man's side a gash. And blood
was sliding softly to the ground.

Next morning by the mud man's side
I was electrified to see
all bisque and beautiful, a bride.
They lay beneath an agate tree.

A serpent made of gems on wire
was coiled along the writhing root
and from the boughs like globes of fire
hung down the blown glass of the fruit.

1947 (?)

(Another, probably a later, form of this poem was included in
Walk Through Two Landscapes; see page 206.)

Last Discipline

They whose strength of bone
has yielded to the grave
where the cumbrous wave
of clay has risen to lave
racked nerves and swirl them down
into the peopled deep,
the unawaking sleep,
for me they keep
through love and its long faith
bond between me and death.

They with their nailed eyes
and their mouths of night
prepare my sight
and curb my tongue aright
for what shall soon arise:
freedom for my ghost,
peace when I need it most.
Through them I am not lost.
What they have dared and done
I'll learn, and not alone.

Where they have gone, I'll go,
and you, who come not yet,
watch where my star has set
but keep your course, and let
no grief have room to grow.
Where I have gone, you'll come.
Death is no less our home
than love is, or the womb,
the sun no less a light
behind earth's cone of night.

1947 (?)

Cross Word-Puzzle

Acerb is sweet,
sharp kind.
Sight belongs
to the blind.

Daffodil's bitter
smell is better
than rose
to the nose.

The hard word
heard
from love's tongue
saves the young.

The rude jest,
parried,
consolidates
the married.

Reject
the compliment,
the kind
intent.

Cherish the
insult, find
strength in the
opposite mind.

1947 (?)

The Good Children

What wisdom suckles them who never doubt the sun—
the animals who wait, polite in dignity,
for no end that we guess, no time to pass?
A picture of a world we would not know
hangs in their antique eyes. Their heads enclose
calm educations we shall never buy.
Their needs so modest, in their miens such patience
as men have lacked since Eve picked knowledge.

1947

The Idols

We climb
timebitten stairs of stone.
From a door at the stairhead
issues a statue,
an idol that stands,
totters, crashes.
About our ankles
roll the crumbs of rock,
frightening but not
bruising us.
We climb.
Another idol follows
the first, breaks,
and we climb.

Another idol.

And we climb.

Though we look neither
to right nor left
fear tells us that the sea
is all afloat with ships,
guns in the ships,
our hearts, our eyes the targets.

Once more the door swings.
The last idol stands,
ancient and hideous and flat,
a Mayan carving
dead and alive.
Her name is Victory.

Thinking of the ships, I say:
"Kneel and supplicate."
We kneel.
Give us the victory, Goddess.

She is deaf. So we climb.
The goddess turns to glass.
Give us victory.
The idol fades,
all but the face, grown beautiful.
It smiles.
And the face thins like smoke
against the grained wood
of the silent door.

Goddess, what have we feared?

(On the manuscript the author has written, "February 20, 1947
[a dream].")

Declaration of War on Me

The war is in myself
and has no pause.
I am my foe
and I defend my cause.

Except myself
no one can harm me
and none as I
can arm me or disarm me.

Except my own to me,
there's no high treason.
To wound as I must wound me
none has reason.

Peace with the world and me
must here begin.
But me I dread
and turn my war within.

1948 (?)

Summer, Be Slow

Summer, be slow to stifle this perfection.
The bare woods are so beautiful, and show
through the thin grille of twigs, in each direction,
the sliding distance and the hill of snow.

The wood now is a birdcage in the breeze.
Its stripped, frail netting lets the eye, as much
as any bird, go searching through the trees.
The wood has August at its fingers' touch

yet holds through April to the rim of June
wedges of winter: snow that binds next summer
to last December, so to importune
time not to toss all to the latest comer.

Sun's warmth we crave—illusion of the south
on north-chilled flesh. But nothing of July,
though it cram strawberries in the willing mouth,
can feed, as April can, the starving eye.

Early 1948

Spheres of Be and Do

The heavy globe is the bones' home, brain's fund,
humus of is, blood's riverbed, and here
energy has a focus. But there turns
another world, impalpable, our life's
insistent reference: the year abides
from fall to fall forever, and the seasons
are fitting quarters for ourselves and time.
Earth spins our atoms and the year our deeds.

1948

Love, without Love . . .

Whirlpool for the eyes
O point of rest
within the vortex, best
loved and desired
spirit I watch you lest
you fly and leave me lost
for I who am nothing
take on a substance
and acquire a root
in the eye seeing me
in the spirit attending:
the attending spirit
empty as I am empty
that takes on substance
and acquires a root
in me, in the eye seeing
the ear hearing the
spirit attending. O love
without love we die.

1948

Monograph on the Grasshopper

I've studied them in various media,
including the encyclopedia,
and gained, from many a thoughtful chapter, a
devotion to the brisk Orthoptera.

The grasshopper has skin to fit
until he grows too big for it.
In danger grasshoppers produce
what children call "tobacco juice."
In grass grasshoppers lay their eggs;
they wear their ears upon their legs.

Now, keep your eyes acutely focussed.
Your grasshopper may be a locust.
(If so, he carries short antennae.)
Saint John the Baptist gobbled many,
though what he gobbled, some have said,
was locust beans, or Saint-John's bread.

In China locusts come in handy;
the Chinese sugar them for candy.
The Arabs grind them, heel and head,
and mix them in their flour for bread.
(It well may be that what the Arob
grinds is the locust bean, or carob.)

Now, men devour the locust form.
But locusts sometimes, in a swarm,
blacken the sky and lick their chops
and vengefully chew up the crops.

Grasshoppers eat young grass and leaves,
bathing suits, play shoes, socks, and sleeves.
True grasshoppers have braided thighs,

they have enormous compound eyes,
they rub the bases of their wings
until they shriek like fiddlestrings.
Half troubadours, half armored knights,
they croon aloud of love's delights.
Each tells his lass the task is hers
to give next spring new grasshoppers.

When spring returns, all thawed and crocused,
katydid, grasshopper, and locust
will prove the claims of the above song
and start rehearsing summer's love song.

Fall, 1948

Words for a Boy

How straight can you stand?
As shipmast or tall tree?
How straight can you look?
Look straight at me.

Neither fumble nor blink
nor feel the least mistrust.
Speak as you think
and act the way you must.

Hurt me? You can't
unless you sell your youth
or look aslant
or speak, and not the truth.

Latter 1940's

Double Projection

I fear that idol which appears alive
between us, gatefaced, one face turned to you
seeming myself, and seeming to be you
the other turned to me. Your fears and mine
marrying in a chasm have made it, a third image
without reality, at work between our loves.
The idol is of air and I can see
through it to you. Look this way. You shall pierce
through it to me, see that I'm not so tall
as it is, not so furious or strong,
but womansized and gentle, like yourself.

Latter 1940's

The Farm Hands

Some whirled scythes through the thick oats.
Others gathered sheaves
and made big ivory wigwams in the sun.

When they went home to rest they had dreams
of grain. The braided ears bruised their eyelids
with remembered shapes. They could not escape
the crops even in sleep.

Latter 1940's

Better Friend

This upright biped is a man.
He's like the famed orangutan.
Astute observers never fail
to note that neither has a tail,
while thoughtful scientists have found
that other parallels abound,
particularly in the brain.
In either case it's all in vain
to teach humanities or math—
they both prefer the primrose path.
If one or other should escape
I'm rather partial to the ape,
and most psychiatrists contend
the ape makes much the better friend.

Latter 1940's

These Are the Past That Is

These are the past that is, their names, their work:
Breughel who props my lids to look at was,
Milton who opens his blind eyes on always,
John Donne, in whose my hand lies quiet in trust,
Blake whose bright statement is a bush of light,
Music, whose name was Mozart, whose dusty flesh
is the shrunk flower of his fruit of work.

Late 1940's (?)

The Fall

All in a wind the world goes
    the wood duck rise and fly
the leaves stream in a storm
    and the stars storm by
        all in a wind all in a wind

Tomorrow comes too soon, too soon
    the mallard cry and go
the northwind sends all summer south
    and the worlds fall and flow
        all in a wind all in a wind

Late 1940's (?)

The Tenth Symphony

Surely the scherzo was ended. But it went on.
Locked in his quiet he had beaten out
the pages to their close. But still there was music.
Voices continued shouting in his head.
The thunder and the waterfall still roared
behind him. An exulting chorus sang
bar after bar beyond the written score.
He wondered if he were going mad, if music
that in his shut brain moved like the sea forever
were lapping his ears from within to shock to action
his muted tympani, absolving him
with a chrism of sound an instant before death.
(Death that might come now if it would. He had worked hard
and was alone and tired.) The great vibrations
harried the podium, wrote upon his skin.
He looked up from his score and suddenly knew
that the orchestra was shouting. The singers clapped
and tears were streaming down the cheeks of some
and some were laughing and pointing fingers at him
telling him to turn around. Fräulein Unger
came forward smiling, took his elbow, turned him about.
And then he knew what movement he had heard,
not his own music, the archangelic shout
of the great Ninth, but what it had evoked:
the cries of thousands of throats, the wind of hands
clapping until they hurt, the stir of feet
clouding old dust into the looped red plush,
the future hailing him, his people
telling him, signing to his moated mind
that he would never die while men could hear
what he had heard beyond his muffled drums.

Late 1940's (?)

Creature

What shall we do with the personal?
Its wings beat in the grasp.

Open the jail of fingers, let it fly in the light.
Where it fluttered in the cage of bones the palms are warm.

Late 1940's (?)

Immediate Freedom

Quartz shadows on the distant floors of snow,
knit with the rosecast of the sinking day,
draw me upon such journeys as I'll know—
and only such. For me there's but one journey—
the one away from me. I cannot go
but where my eye can take my loaded heart
and on the high rock split it clean apart.
The road home, when one lives there, is so far
it spavins courage. I must tread in rings
all the long distance from this close *I am*
to the immediate freedom of *you are.*

Late 1940's (?)

Between

Between the continent of you
and the continent of me
stretches a monster-peopled sea.

Nevertheless, beneath the eels and squids,
foraminifera, silicon, and goo,
there's a connection between me and you.

Late 1940's (?)

Poem

The star watcher may find
it is enough to love.
But I am not so kind.
What moves me I must move
or feel too much alone.
I need the equal glance
to balance mine, the tone
of tongue, man's countenance.

Straight at my side I need
the tall white tree of bone
whose leaves are flesh, whose seed
is human, as my own.
The stars for all their fire
burn but a wintry doom.
I live. What I require
is love and a shut room.

Late 1940's (?)

Dark Death

Dark death, last night I loved you as I lay.
No arms so strong as yours, no kiss so heavy
with peace and mercy and no sperm so swift
as yours whose fruit is silence. All desire
tends to your presence. All the play of love
that lets the senses blaze then die in sleep
is shadow-practice for your best embrace.

Late 1940's (?)

Harsh Trainer

All winter the black elms have risen
from iron earth. Their static streams of fiber
have wedged the arid air, a frozen Tiber,
Amazon, Mississippi, icy prison
of pausing life. Now they begin to flow.
Time that has taught them to be hard and big
whips them again in every new, small twig.
They are old. And yet they hurt with spring. I know.

Late 1940's (?)

Zero

Tall smoke exclaims on the air's stillness.
The sky sings single blue.
Snowfields burn with hickory-keeled feet.
Birdshaken pine trees sprinkle little storms.
The mountains, rouged with sunset snow,
are cold all through.

Late 1940's (?)

(This poem was originally grouped with "Ten Below" and "Twenty Below," pages 16-17, under the title "Three Cold Poems.")

Compost Art

Pattern and paint are in these leaves
as in the cattle in the caves
of Altamira, and they lie
over each other every way
as bison over mammoth rest:
ochre on ochre palimpsest.

Late 1940's

Song of a Sybarite

Tossed by the sea's hand
out of the sea's reach,
shell-petals litter the beach
of skied wet sand.
Time in a blue chime swings from day to night
and every tide is loss.

I've held rose shells like these
assembled into a rose,
but earth's warm petal goes
more swiftly than the sea's.
You love me yesterday and tomorrow
but today I am alone forever.

I shall distract my senses
and deflect my harms
with multitudinous forms
for sure defenses.
I shall eat fragile meat of lacquered crabs
and sunlit saffron melons.

The miscellaneous miracle
of factual creation
shall be the mind's salvation,
its witness and its oracle.
I shall avert despair with stained glass wings
of flies, jade cabbages, hexagonal snow.

Late 1940's

Human Image

The woman with the face of curd
stood in my dream. Her flesh was dead
and yet she lived. She breathed a word.
I have forgotten what she said.

I smelled and saw a bowl of blood
in which with care she bathed a child.
She clothed him with a coat of mud
gently, maternally, and smiled.

Her eyes looked past me, holding fear,
such fear she could not meet my look
lest death should take her mind. Her ear
groped for my meaning, like a hook.

I swooned with pity, though I knew
pity was barbed to wound the dead.
Out of my forehead crept a dew.
I wiped it off. My palm was red.

I touched the child. It shrieked and broke
like a clay doll. I wept   and woke.

Late 1940's

False Move, or Fair

I looked so deep into the pit
my dazzled eyes grew black with it.

The emptiness I sought to plumb
grew up to me, began to come

wave after wave to suck my thought.
Up flew the noose whose name is nought.

The cut stem of an earlier joy
became a withe that could destroy.

O terror! The unbalanced mind
saw death, and wished it had been blind.

All the bells of madness rang:
Leap to the street! Drown! Hang!

I stepped back for a running leap
into the soft womb of sleep.

I stumbled, felt your presence, and
the sane entreaty of your hand.

Late 1940's

Emanation

The poet sweats to build himself a ghost
of words to haunt the world with, lest he be lost
out of the mind of men with his own dust.

Death shall disperse the words, but not so soon,
he hopes, as earth may close about the bone,
or the fierce worm upon his flesh may dine.

He is in love with the mind. There he would fall:
a seed to leaf beyond his funeral;
a bell-note circling broader than the bell.

Stay, my ghost, and claim a slender space
amongst these others. Sleep, my dust, in peace,
if my words breathe an hour above the grass.

Late 1940's

Excursion to the Goddess

Twelve storeys tall, in endless train,
we spiral round the lady's spine
in circulation to her brain—
a human corkscrew, panting line
of curious gazers snailing high,
to wind down to the rock again
from brief promotion to the sky.

Intestinal, the twisting stairs
convey us intimately on
to try the stature Freedom dares.
Like turtles in a marathon
or microbes at their secret murders,
we wriggle through her bolted snares:
the nervous system of her girders.

Seeking to penetrate the core
of Liberty, we are coerced.
Within, we see her rind of ore,
how frail it is, and all reversed,
till through the windows of her crown
the visions of the distance pour
as from her forehead we look down.

Late 1940's

Genetrix

I've waged my long, small war with dream. I'm aged.
Thought and love have aged me, but chiefly love
that stuns the stomach with the huge meal of fear.

A young girl hailed me at the corner of here and yesterday,
my daughter, earlier self, memory of perennial Helen,
Helen, young Aphrodite, proud, keystone of powers.

O rage of time! Long quarrel of the heart with years!
Eros is in the sunlit veins of the young as green is in the branch.
Love is packed like a quince with seeds of grief.
Taste, my child, the bite is sweet, the meal
is hard, but without it you die. Learn what
I cannot teach. Know that I could not ease you.

Late 1940's

Sonnet to a Sister in Error

"Whilst the dull manage of a servile house
Is held by some our utmost art and use."
—Anne, Countess of Winchilsea (1661-1720)

Sweet Anne of Winchilsea, you were no hellion
intent on setting the broad world to rocking.
The long court dress concealed the long blue stocking,
the easy manner masked the hard rebellion.
With light foot stirruped on the Muses' stallion
you ambled privately, afraid of shocking
the Maids of Honor who excelled at mocking
the matchless rose with stitches small and million.

Staunch Anne! I know your trouble. The same tether
galls us. To be a woman and a writer
is double mischief, for the world will slight her
who slights "the servile house," and who would rather
make odes than beds. Lost lady! Gentle fighter!
Separate in time, we mutiny together.

Early 1949

There's Hell, There's Darkness

Persephone has eaten six seeds of the dark fruit
and must keep house in hell for half the year
while Mary wanders in her crown of stars
carrying Kilroy with his million wounds.

Go in peace, good clergy. You have done
right by the parish. Let the clean bells toll.
The full can sleep. The scared can shape their laws.
All's well. Good night. Sweet dreams.

1949 (?)

Ballad of the Bright Hair

Let down your braids, Rapunzel,
pour that gold
that I may take and weave it into shirts
to keep the people from the wounding cold.

      Youth and age
      eternal battle wage.

Leave my braids, Mother.
The young men must attempt
with faith and difficulty these bright ropes.
Man climbs to take the kiss of which he dreamt.

      Age and youth
      look two ways at a truth.

Toss down your heart, Rapunzel,
from your spire.
Bring here the comfort of a daughter's care
and make your brightness a domestic fire.

      Dawn and dusk
      new risen bread and rusk.

Old woman, let me be
and hold your tongue.
A stone wall hangs between us. None can speak
a language common to the old and young.

      Near and far
      how cruel the young are!

Wind your hair, maiden,
up the wall of stone

out of my children's reach, lest they swing up
and leave me in the darkness here, alone.

      Far and near
      the old have grief and fear.

When you are dead, old shadow,
I will climb
down the stone stair, and with my iron hair
weave you a winding sheet—in time, in time.

      Spring and fall.
      Life takes no time at all.

Who then shall lean, Rapunzel,
from your sill,
dropping a ribbon of beguiling fire
to fingers freezing in the moony chill?

      Life and death.
      A word is but a breath.

Silence, old woman!
We shall both be there
rekindled in another who smiles down
and brands the cobbles with her hissing hair.

      Wake and sleep.
      Spend what you cannot keep.

1949 (?)

Protocol

Little girls and little boys,
innocent in all their joys,
gather knowledge crumb by crumb
and NEVER ask how babies come.

When we elders, full of smirks,
tell how procreation works,
theorizing along bee-lines,
pointing out the broods of felines,

little boys and little girls
nod beneath crewcuts and curls
courteously, and never show
that they know we know they know.

1949

Harsh Return

We've put a summer and a sea behind us.
We've left the sun days of the workman months
marooned in yellow yesterday, upon an island
broken out of the year, lopped from hard custom.

To gullscream, herringflash and clap of wood to water
we've promised a return, and traveled inland
and autumnward to fires of stoves and leaves.

We're home to work our passage through to June.
If time be punctual and our courage keep
we shall go back to wear our summer selves
leaving a winter and a work behind us.

September, 1949

Round Song

The children warm our winter like hours of April.
They of the lark mind, the speech of laughing thaw,
crackle the tomb with roots that run like veins.
We are Lazarus, bandaged with an age of days.
They with their Easter hands undo our death.
We are the buried. The world is a clod upon us.
They are the airy morning, a wood of budding birch.
We are the dead. We are the horrible examples.
They are the green resurgence. They are tomorrows,
and confident, difficult innocence of new trials.
They shall be Lazarus, with unbreathing bark.
They shall be swaddled too in a cradle of failure.
They shall be old too, as evening is with no dew risen.
Their children shall warm their winters like hours of April,
they of the lark mind, the speech of laughing thaw,

1950 (?)

Grief of the Trojan Women

Written upon Reading Richmond Lattimore's
Translation of Euripides' Trojan Women

Hector poured
Astyanax
into the mold
of flesh and word

within the womb
the room of love
Andromache shaped
their hope and dream

Troy rocks for cause
too small for God
war eats our nights
death guts our days

Hector is dead
Astyanax
must die. How can
a mother plead?

punish the lamb
and kill the child
proud men gone mad
can feel no shame

we know the grief
of Hecuba
shaking the world
no man is safe

no child of love
is safe, and each

woman is
a weeping slave

Cassandra, come!
yourself a torch
take terrible fire
from Ilion's flame

women! despair
of man's intent.
No more lament.
War on war.

1950–52

The Soul's House

Emptiness is abhorrent to the flesh
but is the soul's house. The poled spirit charges
that wall-less rectangle with all the wit
of the quick mind that was not the fire's food.

Ghost, in your going, you bequeathed us this:
belief in ghosts. We touch the open wall,
receive the shock of what the good call grace.

Date uncertain

How Many Days?

How many days are mine? How long again
shall sky contain me, my mind receive its light
in the presence of my loves?

Yesterday, before the brazen fury of the trumpet
withered the roots of the mountains
and the moon was accused and the sun arraigned for treason

and the stars bombed down from the boughs
of the shaken fig tree of space,
I thought the world fair, and pleasant to dwell in.

But today I find it holy and precious
as a treasure that is forfeit
a privilege about to be withdrawn

and I bless its wounds that I cannot stanch or heal
and I praise it now and forever
in the presence of my loves.

Early 1950

Cuckoo, Jug, Jug, Pu We, To Witta Woo!

Fat and factual robins in the rainy birches
sit all plump and smug and fluff their tangerine chests.
Oh, it is spring all right, it's the only pretty ring time,
and the birds are stealing my gray hairs to line their nests.

All nature is making love, but no, not I.
I'm pushing leaves off the flower beds into potato sacks.
I'm raking the toys and the tinfoil that wintered under the snow,
and the crows are walking around my eyes and leaving tracks.

Early 1950

Therapy

I praise the magic of witches and wizards.
They feed in famines and sleep in blizzards.
They hew to the line that has length, not thickness,
and when I am dying they cure my sickness.

Pah! Aesculapius!—Fie! Hippocrates!
What can you do for me and Socrates?
You can't stop hemlock, you can't lift curses.
Witches are quicker than doctors or nurses.

They fright the tumor they quench the fever
if only you act as a firm believer,
and whether they work from heaven or hell,
God bless the devils that make me well.

Early 1950

Come with Me to Korea, Miss Smith

There are couples on the beach coupling quietly in the sweet warm
    dusk
scandalizing the unlovable who have never coupled
and who hate the soft sounds of love and the sight of the strong
    clinging they haven't known
or have known wrongly and hated. And there are couples
swaying pressed together in the dance halls, drunk with much desire
    and a little gin
but most of all with life, with longing and love of life
and therefore beautiful. The beautiful couples. The couplers.
Bless them always wherever and whoever they are. They do no harm.
The harm is done in the tearing them apart
away from the business of life to the business of death.

Oh Miss Aminta Smith, if you object
to the necking on the beach in the summer dusk,
come with me, do come, to where you'll not be shocked
by the goings on of youth. Come where young limbs lie
quiet. Very quiet. See! There is no lewd motion.
Everything is respectable. Some of these limbs are even
detached from the sinful bodies. Cured of sex.

Summer, 1950

Flowers Out of Rock

Falls of iris and roses stream from the mineral wall.
Hard veins of ruby, diamond, beryl, emerald and gold
soften and sweeten into flesh and flow
over the world, fragrant with death and semen.

Shall we push back stamens and pistils—pack them back
clean and enduring and without odor—precious and secret?
But there is no final keeping. Even the rock is alive
though it dies so slowly under the beak of the wind.

Summer, 1950

Lovesong for Young Oedipus

Youth dreams large and age dreams long
and all a lovetime lives between.
The old no more suffice the young
than leaves of umber match the green.

The North keens and the flocks are gone.
October bleeds. The crocus cures.
Turn from your mother soon, my son,
to kiss a girl with lips like yours.

Fall, 1950

Reality

Flat I fell on the ice—
my head bounced like a ball.
I wondered—did it crack?
I lay there on my back
staring at clouds. How nice!
I didn't mind at all!
It was in fact a spree
to be so toppled flat
from the proud vertical
and made to witness that
the majesty of me
is subject to a fall
sudden and absolute.
Now, that the earth's a true
fact to be fallen to
I can no more dispute.

Date uncertain

The Pull

Man is forever within, forever issuing,
forever seeking exit, but half escaped,
so cold in liberation that he turns
to find the center, to resume the shell.

O love, O terrible force, O dark,
magnetic and beloved earth.

Date uncertain

The Print of Man

Somebody flicked a switch. The trees are lit with green.
Fractions of angels pipe their glee in the branches.
The birds are not concerned with the human condition,
are tongues in Paradise, absolved from our complex pain.

If a bird's life is little, his minute is long, is forever.
No mirror hangs in his head facing a pair of ways
to show him last week's sin, next Tuesday's duty.
Sing, small bodied voice. Your song is all there is of time.

I come to a cave in a mountain and find the relics of angels:
bones of their wings and a shroud that bears the print of man.
I leave the cave, stare down at the cruel cities,
and weeping turn from them to hear the clean birds chanting praise.

June, 1950–January, 1952

Previously
Uncollected
Poems

1951-1960

NOTE

From 1939 to the fall of 1951 all of the poet's published work, in periodicals and in books, was signed *Dilys Bennett Laing*. In October, 1951, as one aspect of a general reassessment of her purposes as a poet, she shortened her professional signature to *Dilys Laing*, which appears consistently upon all of her manuscripts and publications thereafter.

Form

Form begins at the center, seeking bounds.
When roots awaken, words begin, like leaves.
It is withinwardness that tells the surface
what shape to find—what note to strike.

Early 1950's (?)

Ikons of My Self

That all the scattered ikons of my self
may slide one day into a sudden focus
making one breadth and thickness, making one
substance, the substance having essence
and the essence meaning, that these selves
shall meet, unite, expand, explode, and leave
nothing but light, and self-consuming fire,
makes the existence of these little idols
almost to be borne, almost not to be spat upon.

Early 1950's (?)

In Horror of History

In horror of history
the reading spirit shuts the book of wounds
wakes from the dungeon dream.

Who shall rebuke the snake
that in frightful reversal of birth
ingests the living frog?

Who shall arraign God?
Shall men have trial by their peers
and God be tried by men?

Who shall weigh Creation
whose scales of pleasure and pain
keep the perpetual balance?

Is man a sphere of lava, shale, and cloud?
Is man a starved snake
or a strangled frog?

In horror of history
the reasoning angel shuts the book of wars
begs an eighth day of God.

Early 1950's (P)

If it is true that creation is mindless then
mindlessness is a better designer than
mind. It may be that the thoughts of
creation are very very long and slow,
so long and slow that we can't see that
they are there at all.

How the skeleton of a little bat, doll parasol
polished and jointed, wired behind glass in the
biology building, can pierce the eye, mind, heart,
swing wide a window of revelation, of love toward
what we pause before calling God but hope is a
beneficent spirit and believe is a patient maker

and doll parasol is too trivial for this clean core
of onetime flesh, fur and blood, for this central
rectitude of ambient fear and hunger.

Early 1950's (?)

Isaac Is Laughter—Abraham the Tribe

Sins of the cringeing tribe
filth gathered to the goat
exiled on Satan hoofs
to the bone-blanching sands

The ram who bleeds in thorns
evolves to Lamb erect
whose flame of symboled banner
sings from a tilted staff

Lamb spitted on a cross
his fleece all sin and blood
Innocence buys our pardons
from a lofty vendor

The individual pain
redeems the vested calm
The victim has no vote
against the sacrifice

Delegate of our guilt
he spares us as we cheat

Let Abraham smite himself
then Isaac shall go free

Early 1950's

Crucifixation

Jesus Scapegoat,
our lamb crucified,
ram surrogate
and snared in thorn
for all of Abraham's children bound
on the dark hearth of God.

So the victim—
Aztec—Nazi—
slit by obsidian
on the sun's black stone
or oven-burnt
to myths of blood and soil.

So Osiris
sown dismembered,
Orpheus scattered,
Dionysos eaten,
and so an endlessness
of helpless Christs;
whirling Ixions
on axle-trees.

What spirit drools, still famished,
after such bread and wine of dying flesh?
Not God—not ours,
surely—above the expanding cloud,
bribed to forgive our sins by delicate odors
that smoke the troposphere
from towers of pride.

The feast of fratricide is not yet ended.
Neither is our humanity,
O Lambs of all the deadly gods,
begun.

Early 1950's

Is Now

The image is always,
new now and
here now
as it was and shall be:

and the image is a nation and nations
or a company of saints and sinners
a field of folk, a valley of villages,
a catch of phoenixes, a gallows hallowed,
an orchestra, a child, a world, a poem.
Forever different, it flaunts itself's sameness
in lovely variety wooing time to love.

And it is:

the suns and planets turning
you turning to me
we turning to dust
dust turning in light
light turning
turning
always
here and now.

Early 1950's

Picasso's Candlefire

Through the brown candlelight
    I squint and see
      the hoard and sunlight hid from me
under its pyramids of gold.

The blunt knife of the candle
    slits time and shows
      the stairs by which the spirit goes
up or down—I cannot tell.

The candle blinds me still.
    I need the night
      to flood the inner caves of sight
with the black light that roars beyond the prism.

Early 1950's

Alarm

In the serene air the siren
opens like a crack.

Come back—if you care
to live.
Downdelving from the wind
try not to love the sky.

Great insects own it now.

Plough down
to glory in gravel.
See that seeds too
are deeds
if to wait is to do.

When eyesense fails
smellsense and
touchsense grow.

Not seeing stars
we grow them on our noses
and rowel roots.

In, down, and safe—
come quick while you are quick
to graves like saving wombs
while all the upper acres
break into angry waves.

In the serene air the siren
opens like a crack.

Early 1950's

Song for a Nativity

It is a concentrate of fire,
it is a shout within the brain,
within the raging vein, a choir
of birds burning, a green landscape in a barley grain.

Call it poetry, hope, desire,
thirst for truth, or love.
It is a body of grace born in a byre
to which we walk we walk and do not turn or tire.

Early 1950's

Negroes of New Orleans

In black America
the people walk like music

They hold unburdened heads
as if they carried treasure

Pale palms of the dusk hands
clap with a private joy

Pale soles of the dark feet
dance their own way

through streets of stone
among the marble people

February, 1951

Aztec Ruin

Man of dust
man of rag

sick dog—you take
a curbside sleep.

Eyes swivel from you.
How can glass eyes see
a man who looks like dust?

God's image—you?
God's shred and shame.

Where is your house of dung,
you man of ash?

What do you eat?
Stone?

The world's heart is a stone.
Eat it.

Spring, 1951

350

Song of One Burden Bearer to Another

Manuela my dear, give me your water jar.
I would carry it so—like a cool thought above my care—
my arm curved like the handle of an urn,
my hips swaying as if I heard a song.

What Conquistador, young Manuela,
with crucifix or thumbscrew could convert you
from what you were? Eyes of obsidian,
body of supple bronze, you have stepped down
with soft bare foot from your perfidious temple
into the country of the curse. You walk
as if the world were good. Manuela my dear,
give me your water jar.

Spring, 1951

Mexican Hill Farmers

How hard it is to tell your houses from the hills
of dust, O poor and patient! As the brief grass grows
and dies, you do. The wind breathes through your walls,
the smoke breathes out, and every dawn your bones
climb out of sleep to break a little bread
out of the stony mountain.
                              Beside the road
a cross of sticks stands like a holy scarecrow
to frighten poverty and death away
in Christ's name. But the kite wheel in the sun
and the ribbed red dusty carcass of a horse
carries no burdens now across the heartless hills.

1951

Worker

Few things a man needs
to look like God at the hour
        of creation:
white garments, sombrero,
        serape, machete,
and a back that does not break
and a heart that does not break.

1951

Blessed Are the Poor in Taxco

To embrace you as my love suggests,
Señor Peon, Don Pobre y Viejo,
would be to clasp a broken old umbrella,
all skeleton and tatter, and besides,
your old wife might resent the strange señora's
gesture of gentleness—you starveling man
with dusty leather feet and eyes like wounds.

I'd buy, but the car moves. Necessity
drags me away that roots you to the square.
But you have seen the signal in my eyes
and proffer me a basket, with a lost
look of betrayal—and I shape a gesture
begging forgiveness, promising return.

Harsh distance grows between us as a depth
widens between the steamer and the dock
or time between two lovers.

                    Señor Pawn!
Now that I'm back you keep no tryst with me
near the cathedral. Though I trudge and peer
through sun and shadow, under all sombreros,
I do not find you and your hopeful ware,
yet cannot lose you and your hopeless faith.

The image that the retina received
of man forlorn beside the golden church
finds no way out amid the rains of anger.

1951

Yellowstone

Far beneath us eagles wheeled. A nest,
perched on a rocky needle, like a hat
badged with naked eaglets, took our eyes.

Evergreen catfur clothed the slopes that fell
in swooping color to the canyon's foot.
There a green torrent, like a tangled wire,
twanged soundless to our eardrums. Yet, a sound
reached us—another music, such as shells
are empty with: great silence. Looking level,
we saw the sky plunge a viridian wedge
between two cones of indigo and lilac.

The eagles ovaled. From our chip of platform,
stuck like a splinter in the mountain's eyelid,
somebody with a trashbin for a mind
stuttered a beer can, like a dirty word,
into the chasm. The eagles and their shadows
shuttled the air with patterns of disdain.

1951

The Proud and the Humble

I. THE PROUD

Only the saint knows sin how rich it is. The saint
sins breathing, knows that to smell a flower
is carnal and that bread sustains illusion.

The saint is sensual and knows more senses
to sin with than the sinner does. To hear a fugue
offends, since it delights. He cannot flee enjoyment
who when he mortifies the flesh finds that the flesh feels joy
in cease of suffering. The saint is punished
who knows humility to be God's door
yet cannot stoop to it, for lower though he may crawl
than fossil and flint, he carries down and down
unbreakable pride that would refuse all joy
and break all gifts and pit perfected self
against a faulty world. Then death forgives the saint.

II. THE HUMBLE

The poet. He does not ask to be God's peer
but takes earth and makes poems.
The lover. He does as God should do. He loves.
Parents. They work in the mood of God. They make.
Children. They are the creation, experimental and God's own.
Animals. Let the saint watch their humility and patience.
The dust. The dust is without self. No one can blame the dust.

1951

The Poet and His Poem

Look at the weird, non-integrated creature,
quite canceled and subtracted from himself,
prowling the streets and searching for his own meaning.

He thinks himself superfluous: an error
in the community's computing.
Suicide, he thinks, is service to his city.

Yesterday, writing, he was happy and whole.
He had the sense that what he did was good,
nor wished to end a self that served so good an end.

Now, Citizens, what will you give for him?
At his own estimation, not a penny.
He'd give himself away, gladly, to Phlegethon.

But look again. We have a transformation!
Somewhere along the way he stubbed his toe
against his own value. He's wielding a pencil!

Hang out your banners, City! Your poor son,
who thought himself an orphan, beams like a politician
newly elected. He shakes off Lethe

in little drops like a gay spaniel, and he shines
with usefulness. His walk's iambic.
Make way, you bankers, for a busy man!

Late 1951

Dove

When the mind slides behind sleep
it walks into the veins and swims the blood.
The landscape of our nightmare is the flesh.
But seeing that love once paid a nine months' visit
in my dark dust, no dogma can convince me
that holy ghost haunts heaven more than earth.

March 14–15, 1952

Tree Toad

A goblin with
a bubble throat
cracks creation
with a note.

1952

Report of the Dreamer

Conquistador on horseback; he clattered in
through the wide Tudor door. He would not halt.
Breastplate and sword and lance, greaves, plume, and helm,
gauntlets, hooves, mane, nostrils, hocks, and hams
in vast momentum, carved all in one piece
of red mahogany that shone like glass,
and all alive. The visor smiled. The knight
bridled his mount to a snorting stand, then wheeled
and cantered up the mighty stairway, waving.

1952

Big Game

Four giraffes playing Canasta
on four Louis Quinze chairs
at a Boulle table.

The African sunshine is so hot
but this Canasta game is not.

Nevertheless the four giraffes
play pensively with
downcast eyes.

And the lianas sway and hiss.
Not many games are played like this.

April 7, 1952

Comforter

I lost who I was
when fields were freedom
when chains were daisies
and days a chain
and in my since years
in anybody's attic
in everybody's cupboard
I've found no me that fits

The mirror is broken
that showed me a whole face.
Now every glass I ask
answers me a stare.
If God loves jigsaws
I am Her puzzle.
I cannot tinker
my scraps to a soul

Oh where is my me?
When shall I claim it?
Folded on my deathbed
like a crazy quilt?
Then may I wrap me
in patches recollected
and whole as the day's eye
wear myself to sleep

Spring–October, 1952

Proud Parent

What is more nubile than the mind?
It is the marrying kind.

No greedier hungers wake and thresh
through foolish flesh

than keep unhappy thought awake
until daybreak.

In bony caverns child and thought
alike are wrought

and each is thrust with hope and pain
from womb or brain.

Progeny of the intellect
we will protect

with ardor just as quick and blind
as for our earthy kind.

My own ideas are finer far
than all your notions are.

October 5, 1952

The Traveller

He had, he said, passed many sentries
in countries hostile to our hope,
had stopped awhile in some against his will.
He had most feared the folk whose heads face backwards
and tongues speak double, for in their country
they'd held a lynching—no—a crucifixion
followed by a revel. All this the traveller saw,
then, having offered decently to lift
a gift of sour wine to the sufferer's lips,
had barely managed an escape. His face
grew dark as he reported. We saw clearly
how much he feared the memory of that place.

November 20–21, 1952; revised later

Naturalist

FOR DAVID

The talking woods move closer to our lawn
bringing the mad stag and the scented doe.
If farmers mutter at our field of flowers,
find it unfit for horse or cow,
if housewives wonder at our wanton days
spent in scant duty with the mop and hoe

let them inspect the marvels of this house:
tadpoles that twinkle into gleeclub frogs,
newts at their spry aquatic love affairs,
mild snakes that wriggle on our rugs
or suncure in our porch on freshcut boughs,
and captive lives that winnow from their eggs

or pupas, and there lies the cobwebbed jar
that cupped the cricket, and the rusty sieve
that seined the tadpole. All our doors are grass
through which there streams a fugitive
business until the schoolbell wakes and claims
the summer scientist with whom we live.

1952–53

Capsule Dragon

Under the winter water under a freezing stone
the salamander sleeps and is alone.
When April opens the cold locks with narrow keys of fire
what if the salamander chooses to remain
a sculptured symbol of refused desire?

Early 1953

Spring Binding

Out of the libraries the words
flew and pretended to be birds
budding on boughs. Lady librarians,
finding themselves at sudden variance
with desks and rubber stamps, rushed forth
and carolled to the South and North
and warbled to the West and East:
"We are Beauty! Where's the Beast?"

Male readers in the reading rooms,
opening books and finding blooms
instead of printing on the pages,
broke, ramping, into frustrate rages,
rushed out, and, sprouting horn and hoof,
put the good ladies to the proof.
Moral: There's none. Who'll pick a quarrel?
The tale's exclusively immoral.

March, 1953

And Bill Made the Beast of the Earth

The daffodil yellow bulldozer
on the fifth day in May
grandly driven by a gentle chap
in a peaked cloth cap
pushed back the thick green carpet of the field
quickly peeled and flayed the stoneboned land
and
while the strong young driver steered and smiled
piled
like weekday God
the plastic sod
in a wormwarm heap.

Like a brown embryo asleep
half-sensual as at the breach of birth
the effigy of mounded earth
lay in the day in a dream and breathed up steam
prophetic on the tranquil jonquil air.

I the gazer and recorder stood to stare
while brisk bulldozer and pensive engineer
frisked back and forth to make the earth conform.
What could I do with the day
but write its Genesis while they
performed it and the world began?
I know that I fell in love with the peak-capped man
and his daffodil yellow fellow that metal and mind
sculptured a breathing beast for me out of the
                earth's green rind.

Spring, 1953

Atlantic Inland

Amphibian, I fled the sea,
to find it yet in wait for me.

Through foundered hulls of summer's leaves
I climbed the earth to morning's eaves.

High in the whalewalk of the land
I porched my eyelids with my hand

and faced the docklight of the day
that signaled from a mackerel bay.

My shadow streamed behind my sight:
a needle to the destined night.

And all was matinal and pure
and all was inland and secure

till, like a slap dealt from the sky,
an apparition struck my eye:

from valleys, up the morning's side,
the mountains crowded in a tide.

In menace to the frightened brain
a sea flowed where the hills had lain

a sea whose outline graphed a storm
when tumult was the planet's norm

a sea whose tons of sliding salt
came, cataleptic, to a halt.

Within the heaving of that tide
the shipwrecked and the drowning cried.

The hills were gashed with leaning sails
and rainbowed with the spouts of whales

and lofty as the awe of man
the forehead of Leviathan,

a moving fortress, frightful prow,
parted the mountains like a plough.

Fall, 1953

Brother Dog

Bristle-muzzle
puzzle-eyes:
you aim a topaz question
trystfully my way.

Bullseye, my boy!
You read the meter
of the human eye
and know it has caught the flashing
from a mind mapped with trails
of wishing smells.

OUT!

That's the noun in your eye.

I bat it back in speech.
Your rank and young
brute body quivers with a joy
I doubt I often reach
in love or art.

Well—one who suffers
much from walls
knows how it feels
to have a scenting mind.
Take what she offers
though it is not hers.
Your otherness from me,
small brother, dwindles.
Understanding stirs
and kinship kindles
between two breaths.

To creatures of our kind
shut doors are deaths
and windows are false hopes
while glass remains intact.
Freedom's a fact
demanding open doors
for you or me.

Then don't just stand there.
Look! The world is yours.

November, 1953

Holbein Goblin

Dance away from me, Bones,
into that gothic porch I see attached
to a gothic building, attached to a gothic thought,
a doubt of life, a guilt, whose reaching shadow
swings like a nightstick on the sunlit city.
Jesus, comrades, was a healthy man.
Shall he be worshipped dead, a carcass hung,
or believed, living, on the crowded mountain?

1954 (?)

The Hero in Two Metals

With mask of malachite and bones of gold
a man disguised as hero gave my dream
Aztec dimension. Stepping from the sun
he pierced the sleeping kernels of my womb.
I woke and felt the cold kick of my time,
my moonstruck epoch, in my stomach's pit
and saw the hero bringing to my bed
with ruthless ardor, freezing and precise,
his mask of neoprene and bones of steel.

1954 (?)

Episode with an Aphid

I lie in long grass
become a big eye

see a cautious aphid
six-legging it down a grass bannister,
looking, before he creeps,
with eyes like black-pepper-motes

Translucent green baby
all alone in the cosmos
with a face not motherloved

Though God may not, I notice him
but does he notice that?

Lucky I'm not a hungry ladybug
not even a lady

With so much in common
what mates we could be!

We both eat sleep pair walk
apprehend falling love sun
and grass live for the moment
are scorned by true gardeners
and both on honey-dew are fed
and drunk

O Aphid! Repository of
unachievable comradeship!

Our incompatability
is a matter of millimeters

Also I fear
I'm a little too old for you

1954 (?)

Ah!

It must be simply thrilling
to live with a poet
the lady said,
giving me an
innocent
Lesbian
ogle.

Madam—have you ever lived
with a tiger?—or a
bitch in heat?
I mean—excuse
me, but you
make me
giggle.

Early 1954

*Easter

FOR EVE, MY MOTHER

Redemptive fingers of the goddess turn
the key that shifts the tumblers. Toward the tomb
three figures walk in frieze, as on an urn,
to claim their remnant of official doom.
But love has still another grief to learn:
stalactite in the grave's abandoned gloom
only the seraph seems to hang and burn.

Twice put in jeopardy and both times caught,
they stand condemned. Love has escaped their care.
But, cast to earth like corn, he has been brought
to rise again: green bread upon the air.
The angel fades like a nocturnal thought
at morning, and the women run to share
the tidings of the joy his lips have taught.

She who has weighed the women and their grief
moved with the angel past the portal stone
and at the icy root unlocked the leaf
in secret, so that death was overthrown.
She is the treasure's keeper and its thief.
Hers is the name with which the rock is sown,
whose lilies are the bells of our belief.

February–March, 1954

Eastre: Anglo-Saxon goddess of spring.

Springclean

A pride of housewives from the granite hill
mounted their next-to-Godly brooms
and scurried to the scrubbing of the Spring.

On all the landscape's buntinged rooms
they poured the contents of their discontent:
a scouring powder harsh and quick.

They'd housebreak Cerberus. What Ceres meant
was never neat enough for dusting wives
who'd drown the yellow elm in lemon oil.

Chopping the heart as fine as chives
to season salads, rinsing out the roots
with bleaching fluid, flicking off the gold

from jonquil eyes, good women in cahoots
with tidy death rub April clean as bone.

Spring, 1954

Letter to the Prioress from a Lay Sister

Mother Theresa   you yourself have said it:
The Way of Perfection is for me as well.
But if I seek it for my poem?   Tell
if Heaven will allow me some small credit.
Can I, in other words, improve and edit
me, through my poem, safely out of Hell?

No?   Lady Prioress   I've often noticed
how under your good humor and your tact
your heart is strict as justice.   Truth's a fact
not lenient to desire.

                    I mark your protest
but, murmuring "Servat homo id quod potest,"
damn self   to save my poem in the act.

1954

The Catch

There was an eagle in his house
loudening all the corners of his rooms
with wingbeats, pouring such a shine
on all his bric-à-brac that it appeared
like driftwood on a beach at dawn.
His neighbors cried along the wire: "We'll come
and douse the fire!" But when they flocked and found
the blaze within to be God's messenger
striking his standard at the mortal roof
they clashed their pails and ran the other way
piously crying: "Crazy—crazy—crazy!"
There was a wrangle then of arms and wings.
And in a hundred years the people came
to show the spot where he had caught the eagle
with words that had become the speech they used.

1954

(Written upon the completion of Alexander Laing's *Jonathan Eagle*.)

Water

In the night the tactile night
I waken blinded by obsidian light

lie beside you all alone and crave
a Eucharist to quell the inner wave

of chaos, wine or wafer that can feed
the marriage-thirst for life. Dry fibers need

a sip of crystal. Cylindered in sand
made lucid, here is water at my hand

now at my lips. I take the liquid bite
that brings me absolution from the night

and fall forgiven to the door of light

1954

Birth of a Saviour

Fathered by a feather
falling in a ball
Humming-Bird-Wizard
was immaculately bred.
Snake-Skirt-Woman
sweeping the temple
saw the pretty spheroid
swirl above her head
popped it in her huipil
and went on sweeping.

Snake-Skirt-Woman
Mother of the South Stars
knew she was pregnant
and felt a bit alarmed.
Huitzilopochtli
embryonic warlock
deep in the world-womb
was busy getting armed.

Snake-Skirt's daughter
Painted-With-Bells
summoned her brothers
and cried out: Shame!
Matricidally
down the South Sky
Snake-Skirt's children
furiously came
all four hundred
hooting her name.

One star-brother
guessing at godhead
driven by guilt-dream

fled to warn.
Snake-Skirt listened
to his tale of treason
so did the feathered One
yet unborn.

Courage, Mother!
piped Huitzilopochtli—
I'll kill my brothers
for calling you a whore.
I'll kill my sister
and a whole lot more!
Hummingbird-Wizard
sprang from the world-womb
fully armored
and brandishing a snake
and he killed the whole family
for his mother's sake.

Huitzilopochtli's
terrible pyramids
blaze with blood
in the sun's humming light.
Brave young warriors
fine in feathers
lose their hearts
to the God of Fright
lose their souls
to the Sun Arising
who puts the Stars
to deathly flight.

Huitzilopochtli
Aztec darling
God of disguises,
victims, war,
they bake his idol
of blood and cornbread

they eat the body
that they adore.

Huitzilopochtli!
Shout it all together!
His mother is immaculate!
His father is a feather!

1954–55

New Saw

Woman's place is in the kitchen
bitchin.

Middle 1950's

For It Is Better to Marry than to Burn
—I Corinthians 7:9

Let us not disparage
marriage.
Even Saint Paul
after all
held that it was better to be tied
than fried
(or so he said in a release
to Greece)
and a real man will prefer
a her
to having sex
vex.
Much depends on whether a man
can.
Probably abstinence
makes sense
putting him in the proper attitude
for beatitude.
But he who is even half alive
should wive
even though (and here's the size of it)
he dies of it.

Middle 1950's

To Members of a Holy Order

Adorable beasts   apologists of life
whose argument is made by glance and posture
who tell by motion and symmetric look
the truth of pattern flowing in infinite change

O furred apostles   finned and taloned priests
living in faith of being   without complaint.
Let other saints learn discipline from you
who make no claim but move within your law.

Middle 1950's

Cocklebread Song

O estrogenic urge of aim
and birthpangs of the psychic tree!
Minerva amputates her name
and swallows ergot for her gree.

Where rabid spandrels dare impinge
sebaceous boarders, armed with pails,
follow the ream, and do not cringe,
but take the blame their deed entails.

Rapt gallimaufreys, pent in pews,
incriminate the immaculate yen
and claymores do themselves amuse
by clinking inklings in the glen.

When in the ogives of the deep
marmoreal girders bind the spray
the galliard and the grommet sleep
and prim euphorias pine away.

The millepora, trained to chime,
complete their triumph, stress on stress,
projecting on the targe of time
a lion jessant of a fess.

Nimbly the young gazebos graze
in pastures where the grilse incline,
while the porbeagle ends its days
echoic, turbid, and condign.

Middle 1950's

Metamorphosis of Rimbaud

He dreamed a caterpillar dream
of wings.

While we waited for more words
he leapt and vanished
in an aurora of flying.

We smelt the singe of sun.

Middle 1950's

Song for a Tribe

Great continent
America of the North—

all directions yours,

America of the calms and spaces
America of freedoms and choices

where no hurry nor huddle
where no greed or fear need be,

the great guiltless beauty
of the earth of our country

spreads past the compass
of the single eye.

Tremendous, bountiful,
millennially strong

O that your children
would create themselves

in your image!

Middle 1950's

Manfight

Haloed with eyes, coquettish as a girl,
the young Torero summons all his wit
to pose at the completion of a twirl
and in his rose bolero stitched with pearl
waits like a ballerina for the burst
of adoration from the gods and pit.

Now the bull gathers, seven festive darts
wagging like wings above his bloody nape.
The mob roars: Olé! Olé! and the thirst
mounts for a death. Felipe has their hearts
but the bull, also, wears a crimson cape.

Middle 1950's

Now

Short shadows
and raised clock-hands
proclaim the noon
I'm locked in.
Yesterday we kissed.
But that was yesterday.

Middle 1950's

Veterans

Women receive
the insults of men
with tolerance,
having been bitten
in the nipple
by their toothless gums.

Middle 1950's

The Dilettantes

Between the blown hills the white, speeding hulls
burn silver in the lake's reflected fire.

Tilted, we ride the water, rein the wind,
and feel the sky's hand in our pennant hair.

Our serious purpose is to know delight
while frivolous statesmen set our course for fright.

Middle 1950's

Time of Ruin

Into the black immoderate waters
bleeding out of the body of our hate
the reasonable cities break like bread.

Love that has cried out and not been answered
hides its hunger with a snarl.

Men who cannot forgive themselves
punish the unwary world.

Middle 1950's

For What We Are About to Receive

Suck this lemon—
this green persimmon,
they're all you'll have
from cradle to grave.
Don't make a face.
Say grace.

Middle 1950's

Fertility Rite

Children are hanging
in the black cathedral
ten thousand children
on strontium crosses.

The floor is slippery
with blood and milk.
The priests pronounce it
a good sacrifice.

They say the children
wept without control
making good augury
for rain and crops.

High in the cracking cupola
the mosaic eyes
of archangels and saints
weep fire.

Middle 1950's

Forgive Me

Forgive me for neglecting to show you
that the world is evil.
I had hoped your innocence would find it good
and teach me what I know to be untrue.

Forgive me for leaving you open to persistent heartbreak
instead of breaking your bright heart with medicinal blows.
I had hoped your eyes would be stars
dispelling darkness wherever you looked.

Forgive me for a love that has delivered you
unwarned to treachery. Now I confess that the world,
more beautiful for your presence, was not fine enough
to warrant my summoning you into it. My beloved.

Middle 1950's

Aquitation

My little boat
galloping on the lake
tugs at its reins.

Crazy colt,
it scampers past
flags of cloud.

The luff of my sail
thrums
in the eye of the wind.

Tiller to boom,
I turn and canter lightly
to hitch at a mooring.

Middle 1950's

Return to Strangeness

Remembering maps we think the road unchanged
but taking it again we make a different journey

Same names of valleys highways hills and selves
but on the slopes another season   other flowers
while in the twiggy orchards of our nerves
time is transformed in bitterness and grace

Nothing is ever twice   not even what we mean
when   too much trusting language   we repeat
names that have gathered to themselves new truths
of ancient knowledge lately found

January 26–March, 1955

The Poets

Joy hinges knees of boys and girls
and makes their hands the gates of music.

The tears of children, spilling on the sand,
widen into pools of singing frogs.

The lions from the jungle of the child
walk through walls and scorn the doors and windows.

Children know Time isn't true. The clock
is a trap the grownups use for wounding Now.

May 24, 1955; revised later

Ignis Dominae

Whoever, by whatever strife or luck
struck it for me—this glint

from flint or stick—whatever
quick Prometheus or

jutmuzzled stoneage physicist
persisted from smallboy urge to try and see—to toast

and taste—I have it now, captive
in my adaptive kitchen

a witch's gift
swift to brew eye of newt or

toe of frog or tongue of beef
chief of all helps to woman

keeper of hearths—
still Vestal though not virgin.

1956 (?)

Maintenant

Over gold lilies in the dusk
a lemon moon drips antique honey
and time is in the hand.

The loved and loving are together
with human intellect and vision
to apprehend the spell.

Hemlock, willow, birch, and elm,
like holy sisters—nuns or dryads—
signal past the eye

and past the ear the frogs declare
a credo of desire, a power
of passion over death.

Earth is a room. When faith is tenant
the resurrecting year ensures
a habitat for love.

June, 1956

(A longer and probably later form of this poem, entitled "The
Grove," appeared in *Poems from a Cage;* see page 6.)

Ring Time

The crow chides. The sudden ember sun
heaves above the cindered hills.

The hard caws hack at memory, revive in me
childhood's firebug joy at kindled day.

In cheer of mind I break from bed to window:

the ragged wings, a tatter of the dark,
flap from the field—a shadow torn away
from strips of night streaming from tree roots.

Peremptory waker—he calls more than his clan—
he circles me to innocence again
from lethargies of time. I stand erect
and listen for a half forgotten order.

The bright black captain rises, cawing commands.
The dew flings glittering from his brisk wings.
The risen sun smites his coal to iris fire.
He dips to a pine. The branch dances.
Trees all around shake with his hidden cohorts
who startle April with astringent greetings
and cancel forty of my fifty winters.

("Completed Oct. 29, 1956, after many revisions. The idea based
on a vivid memory of experiences at the age of ten."—D.L.)

Fragment

You warn of hell but do not know my hell.
I warn you: do not come here. It is private
and worse than any hell of which you tell.

1957 (?)

Age of Unreason

If there's anything worse than the machine age
it's the teen age.
Parents and teachers agree among themselves that it's the mean age.

Those who are in it
are not agin it—
they seem to work at being that way every minute.
It's only those who've left it far behind
who mind,
and wonder if the teenager is human after all or a member of some
other kind.

It's a question whether the teenager has a soul
or just nerves that rock and roll.
When you speak to one, even though he's near you,
he doesn't hear you,
not just because he's listening to built-in jazz—
it's the crazy ideas he has
such as: his parents don't understand him
and *their* crazy ideas will socially brand him.

Adult theories of dressing
he finds depressing.
If you tell him timidly that the seat of his pants is tearing
he answers that that's what the cats are wearing.
He thinks that everyone over twenty
has lost life's plenty
and considers a tot of twelve or under
a cosmic blunder.
We who have recovered from being teenagers can't recall
what it was like at all.
It's a seizure, an amnesia, a catalepsy
of bop and pepsi
and if you don't have it you're not hep, see?

As an absolute pre-requisite to mating
there's dating
which usually consists of waiting
and ends in hating.
But the business that makes parents moan
is the phone.
Every teenager really ought to have his own.

If you venture any kind of advice
the teenager turns to ice,
or his face assumes a look of prudery or nausea as if your views were
    not quite *nice*,
because (and he doesn't actually say this in case he'll hurt you)
he has his own ideas of virtue
which have nothing to do with *your* ideas of law and rule,
but as far as he's concerned, they're cool,
and if you don't think so then *you* know who's a fool.

You have the gnawing sense that perhaps you could teach him
if only you could *reach* him,
while he thinks he could learn everything perfectly well
if only you would go to bed.

1957 (?)

Carol to Be Sung to Lutes or Banjos
WITH RESPECTS TO PIERO DELLA FRANCESCA

Angels strum their lutes and carol.
The ass brays tenor the ox moans bass.
Joseph sits on an upturned barrel.
Shepherds are kneeling all over the place.

> Oh everything's gone turntable,
> even the stars run wild.
> There's a new little calf in the stable.
> *They say it's a human child.*

The innkeeper's wife while making the beds up
hears the news, goes out to check.
The ox and the ass are sticking their heads up
singing like mad. With bended neck

> the mother looks at her baby
> who laughs on straw soft-piled.
> The innkeeper's wife thinks maybe
> *it's more than a common child.*

Oh let all kings come make obeisance
and let all beggars come find their joy.
The world was old but here's renaissance
come in the guise of a hayseed boy.

> Herod fumes at his danger.
> Names are gathered and filed.
> That carpenter's chip in a manger—
> *They say it's a royal child.*

Men and angels shout the sequel.
The birthday of the world begins.

Kings and shepherds all are equal,
rose or plum or nut their skins.

When Cain takes care of Abel
the serpent is beguiled.
Love is born in a stable.
They say it's a holy child.

1957

Pius Thought

"No one can say woman is inferior . . . never-
theless wives must submit themselves to
their husbands as the Church does to
Christ."—Pope Pius XII, UP, Oct. 2, 1957.

Woman—said the twelfth of his name piously
(and his fiat ringed the earth)
was by God created equal with man
in dignity and worth.

Nevertheless—said he—the Convert preaches
that woman must be humble and mute
and lay her down under the burden of man
and be his brute.

Early October, 1957

Storm Near Lesbos

                        You stood in my doorway
a lighted flower a singing tree charged with a feeling
you mistook for thought   a passion you mistook for
worship   the lantern of your flesh flooded with rose
and I blushed in secret at being so overvalued
                                          and
unwisely I said I love you   and it is true I loved and
love you as I love all innocence
                        and you shook and wept
so that I comforted you for a moment in my arms and
thought of the isles of Greece and trembled and let you
go
      no   sent you away since going was not in your mind
or power
              and now I remember you as I remember my own
innocence and as I recall the dignity of childhood and
the unbearable sweet solemnity

Mid-October, 1957

I-Thou

Dear God
if it is true
that you made me
in your image
you must be
an agnostic.

1957

Penalty of Excellence

Some of the best are dead and some not born.
A few live who are good, a very few
live who are wise. The best of men have peers
only in other epochs than their own.
It is the penalty of excellence
to have a century to burn alone in.

Late 1957

Next-to-Godliness

God so loved the Spin-Dry world
he gave Divinity
to Cleanliness.

Hungrier for goods than Good, we know
that happiness can be pursued,
bought, and put in the Deepfreeze.

God sits in the refrigerator.
His votive light goes on and off
as the shrine door swings.

He acts through the Dispose-All
that this corruptible
may put on incorruption.

Ask, and it shall be given you;
seek, and ye shall find;
knock, and it shall be opened unto you.

A godly folk, we always get what we want.
Just now we want to be
Men-in-the-Moon.

1957–58

Final Verdict

The Prisoner is pronounced guilty in the First Degree.

In the unique position to give aid and succor
he remained aloof.

Seeing the children drown he did not throw them a line.
He saw the railroad bridge wrecked by the flood and did
not warn the engineer.
He stood by while a maniac used and destroyed a little girl.
He saw his own son lynched and did not interfere nor
protest nor bring the murderers to justice.

Asked what he has to say he makes no reply.
He is sentenced to burn in a bush.

Latter 1950's

God
has gone
out of the sky
to make space for men

Latter 1950's

Note

What is a poem?
It is what a man is: a periphery
of something central and unseen.
The neutral, the cerebral beast;
the verbal form
are the mind of the storm
and the center is silence.

Date uncertain

Statics of Composition

Not
landscape alone
not
man alone
but the human person
near the windtorn tree

Latter 1950's

Losing Game

Actaeon in the baying wood
has chanced on Virtue bare.
That he must die is all the good
he got from such a stare.

Antlers upon his brow are bossed.
Virginity's so dread
that maidenheads before they're lost
can horn the hunter's head.

Latter 1950's (?)

I put down my book
The Meaning of Zen
and see the cat smiling
    into her fur
as she delicately combs it
    with her rough pink tongue.

"Cat, I would lend you this
    book to study
but it appears that you have
    already read it."

She looks up and gives me
    her full gaze.
"Don't be ridiculous," she purrs.
    "I wrote it."

Latter 1950's

Miao: excellent, mysterious, subtle.

Prayer of an Ovulating Female

I bring no throat-slit kid
no heart-scooped victim
no captive decapitated
and no self-scourged flesh.

I bring you, Domina,
Mother of women,
a calendula in a pot
a candle and a peach
an egg and a
split condom.

Ave Mater
Mulierum!
may no blood flow
nec in caelo
nec in terra
except according
to the calendar.

Latter 1950's

Explaining van Gogh

A blue sun pulses in my sky of blood
as I lie eyelidded against the light—
a kingfisher in a red sea, a peacock in a bonfire,
simulacrum of nature, not natural, but true.

Vincent, dazzled by the sky of Arles,
saw so, eyes shut against custom,
and so dazzled us.

Latter 1950's (?)

Nature and Human History

The clean snow seen through our window
yesterday held for me no meaning.

Today I see your footmarks
making a long chain into the pines.

Latter 1950's

The Husking

As blind as any shedding snake
I slept ten circuits of the clock
then peeled my skin off like a shirt
and left it hitched upon a rock.

And when my eyes could bear the light
I tasted time with slitted tongue
and knew the hungers I had known
a skin ago when I was young.

1958 (P)

414

Stabat Mater

In love's long execution she
is fixed upon the human tree

The tree is fashioned like a cross
the cross is image of her loss

Loss and cross and tree are one
in the person of her son

In her hands the wounds are wide
in her feet and in her side

and since the day that he was born
she has felt the stabbing thorn.

1958 (P)

Freshman

His face is like a girl's, heartshaped
and beardless. He would like to seem
more weathered than he is. But how?
Puppies betray with silky coats
and bungling paws they are not dogs.

Grandmothers see their sons in him,
grandfathers their own early strife,
matrons would love to pamper him,
girls to marry him, and teachers
to shine their honor through his mind.

But he is wary of them all.
Only one thing can help him: Time
that hardens saplings into logs
and wrings the girl-face of a boy
into the old man's anguished mask.

1958–59

Prescription (Obsolete)

There's someone fumbling in the lab,
who, businesslike in gloves and mask,
dissolves the planet in a flask.

Try to recall one gentle thing
we knew (before we all drop dead):
"Love one another," someone said.

Early 1959

Checkmate

I live with my animal
my savage mirror mate.
Hairy sebaceous and eructive—
still it is warmer than death.

I house with my animal
which, gourmandizing
self relieving and lusting
pricks my pomposities
and makes a plain journey.

I boast to my animal
that I have loftier aims.
It jeers at me from the glass, agrees
that death is trustworthy
as a destination.

April, 1959

Threnody on the Demise
of As and Now

Forgive me
while I drop
a gentle tear.

Presently,
now is dying.
So is *as*.

(Not *dying*,
but obsolescent,
like we say

in all the
leading papers
presently.)

Proximately
soon will be
extinct

like a door-
nail, like as
and now

sure are
gonna be dodos
proximately.

Parm me
pliz while
I exude

a modicum of
lachrymal
secretion.

1959

The Swift Ships

Under the jet sawn sky
I think of Greece—
her blood-bright sea whose waves
beat on the shores of our civility,
and, loud with the beginnings of our peace,
were slashed to foam by slaves.

Late 1950's

Fragment

Sleep, soft murderer, antique subversive ghost
lying in ambush in the primal fern,
black force that is my self's own darkest tide
climbing to drown the island of my thought,
footpad sleep—stalking daylit hours
with anesthetic threat

Late 1950's

Translations
Not
Previously
Collected

Fall

(From the German of Rainer Maria Rilke)

As from afar the leaves come down—as though
distant gardens withered high in heaven;
the leaves drift down with gestures of denying.

And in the night the heavy earth falls flying
from all the stars to loneliness below.
So we all fall. This hand falls. See how all
others are falling also. Nothing stands.

Yet there is one who softly in his hands
holds through eternity this endless fall.

1950 (?)

The Chase of the Child

(From the French of Jacques Prévert)

Bandit! Blackguard! Scoundrel! Thief!

Birds above the island flutter.
Around the island there is water.

Bandit! Blackguard! Scoundrel! Thief!

What on earth is all that yelling

Bandit! Blackguard! Scoundrel! Thief!

It is the pack of decent men
out hunting down the child

He'd said I've had enough of the reform school
The guards smashed in his teeth with keys
And left him stretched on the cement

Bandit! Blackguard! Scoundrel! Thief!

Now he has escaped
And like a hunted beast
He scurries in the night
And hot upon his heels
Come cops tourists artists stockholders

Bandit! Blackguard Scoundrel! Thief!

It is the pack of decent men
out hunting down the child
No license needed for this hunt
All honest people may join in
What is that swimming in the night

What are those flashes and those bangs
It is a child who runs away
It is the noise of rifle shots

Bandit! Blackguard! Scoundrel! Thief!

All those gentlefolk on the shore
Are jabbering and green with rage

Bandit! Blackguard! Scoundrel! Thief!

Back to the continent at once

Birds above the island flutter
Around the island there is water.

Latter 1950's

Place of the Merry-go-round

(From the French of Jacques Prévert)

At the place of the merry-go-round
at the close of a fine summer day
the blood of a horse
hunched and harnessed
trickled away
over the paving
and there was the horse
waiting
quite still
on three of his feet
the other foot wounded
wounded hanging
and trailing
and close at his side
waiting
quite still
there was the driver
and there was the carriage waiting quite still
as useless as a broken clock
And the horse kept quiet
he didn't complain
he didn't neigh
he stood there
whiling time away
so reasonable so fine so grave
so simply brave
how could one keep the tears back?

Lost gardens
forgotten fountains
sundrenched plains
oh lustre, pains

and mystery of adversity
brightness, blood
and beauty stricken
Oh brotherhood.

Latter 1950's

The Rose of the Infanta

(From the French of Victor Hugo)

The little one and her duenna stand
at the pool's edge—a rose in the child's hand.
The small girl gazes. What is it she sees?
She scarcely knows: the birches and pine trees
darkening the water, a slow swan, the dance
of waves beneath the fiddling boughs; her glance
sweeps the deep, alleyed garden, all aflow
with flowers. She seems an angel formed of snow,

and sees a palace as in a burst of rays,
a park, bright fishpools where deer drink, the blaze
of peacocks in the wood, like gems in hair.
Her innocence is a whiteness over her.
All her small graces are a sheaf that shakes.
The splendid grass surrounding her awakes
with flash of ruby, spark of diamond.
The dolphins' mouths spit sapphires in the pond.

Enchanted with her flower, there she stands
mirrored, her overskirt is rich with bands
of Genoa lace, her skirt is Florentine
with threading gold throughout its rippling sheen.
The full-blown flower, bursting and upborne
from its green cup as from an open urn,
loads the bewitching smallness of her hand.

She pouts her charming lips, and, petal-skinned,
wrinkles a laughing nose, sniffs the perfume
of the magnificent and royal bloom.
Half the small face behind the blossom hides,
so that the eye must pause while it decides
whether it be the child or flower that shows

and if it see the rose cheek or the rose.
The pure dark eyebrow heightens the eyes' azure.
She is all delicate scent, enchantment, pleasure.
How blue her glance!—Mary how sweet a name!
All gleams—her name a Hail!—her eye a flame.
And yet—poor innocent—she feels the weight
of being one among the very great.

She's witness to the spring, to light, to shade,
to the magnificence the sun has made
across the horizon with its vanishing beams.
She hears the chattering of invisible streams,
gazes upon the calm, immortal scene,
presiding gravely, like a little queen.

She sees no man but with his back aslant.
She'll be, one day, the Duchess of Brabant.
Flanders, Sardinia, will be hers. You see
the Infanta, five years old, all dignity.
The fragile foreheads of kings' children wear
a ring of shadow. Their tottering first steps are
the beginning of a reign. She smells her flower
waiting to pluck an empire. Royal power
already in her glance, says: This is mine.
Love, mixed with terror—subtle as a wine—
flows from her. If someone seeing her so small
should reach in pity to save her from a fall,
before he takes a single step, or speaks,
he feels at his throat the dark threat of the axe.

Now the child smiles, does nothing but to pose,
to live, to hold in her small hand a rose,
under the heaven, in the midst of bloom.

Day dies. The twittering nests are quarrelsome.
The sunset dyes the trees. Its colors flush
the marble goddesses until they blush

and seem to tremble as the dusk draws in.
All wingèd things come down. No flame. No din.
Mysterious evening gathers the sun safe
beneath the wave, the bird beneath the leaf.

The child laughs, flower in hand. And in the great
palace whose pointed arches catch the light
like mitres, a dark form behind the panes
moves deep in shadow, by some shadowy means,
from window to Gothic window, striking fear
into what mind may see it lurking there.
This very shadow, like a ghost that grieves
near tombs, stands sometimes there all day, perceives
nothing, but seems to pass from room to room
alone and ghastly in the oppressive gloom.
Pressing its brow against the panes, it dreams.
Its shadow lengthens in the sunset's flames.
It walks as if it heard a death-knell ring.
And it is Death. Unless it be the king.

It is the king; in whom the realm exists
and trembles. Could some watcher read this ghost's
eye, where he leans there, shoulder against the wall,
he'd see in that abyss no rose, no small
Infanta, nor the pool brocaded by
the gold reflected from the evening sky,
and not the arguing birds, and not the grove.
But in the eyeball's secret glassy wave,
under the fatal eyebrow that keeps screened
the brooding pupil, sea-dark and profound,
this is the moving image he would find:
a flight of vessels running before the wind,
and, in the foam and folding waves, the pale
huge quivering of a great fleet under sail,
and there, beneath the fog, an island rock
receiving the ship's waveborne thundershock.

Such is the vision that can be defined

in the cold caverns of this prince's mind,
blinding his vision to what is near at hand.
He sees his conquest of a coveted land.
And the Armada, fulcrum of the lever
with which he is committed to turn over
a world, sails on. He sees with his mind's sight.
His tragic boredom has no other light.

Philip the Second was an accursed man.
Cain in the Bible, Iblis in the Koran
are not so black as in the Escurial
this spectral son of the imperial
spectre. He was evil with a sword—
the dream of evil and the high world's lord.
He lived. And no-one dared regard him. Fright
gave him an aura of inverted light.
Only to see his stewards passing used
to make men tremble, since their minds confused
Philip with the abyss or with the stars,
he seeming one of God's familiars.
His desperate will, deep-seated, obstinate,
was like a grapple fastened upon Fate.
He held America, the Indies, leaned
on Africa. England alone remained.
His mouth was silence and his soul unknown;
fraud and deceit the substance of his throne;
equestrian statue on a shadowy horse.
The powers of night imbued him with their force.
Always attired in black, he seemed to mourn
himself. And, like a sphynx whose thoughts are borne
in silence, saying nothing there he stood.
No-one had seen him smiling, for how could
those iron lips have smiled? One might as well
hope to see dawn at the black gates of hell.
If ever he shook himself behind his mask
it was to help the hangman at his task.
He was a blight on progress, on man's hope,
on life, on law, but faithful to the Pope.

He was the devil reigning in the name
of Christ. From his necrophilic nature came
viperlike horrors, writhing and spectral.
In Burgos, Aranjuez, the Escurial,
his palaces stood dark. He saw no reason
for levées, feasts, and clowns. His jest was treason,
burning of heretics and Jews his sport.
Kings trembled in the night at the report
of Philip's hatching plans. And like a curse
his plotting weighed upon the universe.
His power and purpose were to break and plunder.
His praying had the groan of muffled thunder.
Lightning flared from his nightmare. Those to whom
he turned his thought felt stifled by a doom.
The people cringed beneath his smouldering scowl.

Charles was the vulture. Philip was the owl.

The golden fleece on his black doublet flamed.
Fate's frozen sentinel one might have named
the king, who, dangerous in stillness, stood
spying on life, as from a cave or wood,
with blazing eyes. His finger seemed to draw
swiftly a secret gesture no-one saw,
vaguely to write an order to his vile
collaborators. When he essays a smile,
grudging and bitter, it is because there flowers
vast in his mind the symbol of his powers:
his army moving grandly on the ocean
as if his own breath set it all in motion,
as if he hovered at the zenith there
moving it with his will's impulsive air.
All's well. The sea grows gentle, quelled in mood
by awe of the Armada, as the Flood
was by the Ark. The vessels are arrayed
in a fixed pattern, like a chessboard laid
with all its pieces. The king's questing eye
sees from the vantage of his spectral sky
decks, bridges, masts, all heaving like a net

spread huge upon the ocean's restless fret.
These ships are cherished. Sentient waves contrive
to hedge about them. That they may arrive
swiftly, the currents all conspire to move
the seaborne army. Winds with protective love
impel it to its ports. Reefs move aside
in courtesy. Foam falls in pearl. The tide
favors these ships. Now let the English fear
each galley guided by its pioneer.
Ships of the Scheldt, of the Adour, they are
speeding with all the panoply of war,
their hundred colonels and their two commanders.
Here are the hulls of Germany and Flanders,
from Naples brigantines, from southern Spain
galleons. From Lisbon sailors, fighting men.
And Philip hovers. What is space? He hears
and sees. The speaking-trumpets in his ears
tell triumph. Cries of sailors and the rap
of drums delight him. Bent above his map,
the Admiral ponders. Signal whistles shriek.
The ghostly hubbub rises to a peak.

And are these cormorants? Or citadels?
Like huge wings beating are the enormous sails.
The water growls. The vast group scuds and flies
and swells and rolls with prodigies of noise.
The king grins as his ghostly eye regards
four hundred ships and eighty thousand swords;
grin of the vampire sucking his black wine.
Philip exults: 'Lost England! You are mine!
For who can save you now? The match is lit
to touch the powder. Who can hinder it?'
He grasps his sheaf of lightning. Who can twist
these blazing bolts from his convulsive fist?
He is the heir of Caesar and the lord
none crosses. He is Philip of the sword,
whose shadow sweeps from Ganges to the spur
of Posilipo. Who shall dare demur

against his wish? Is it not he who takes
Victory by the hair? and he who makes
these terrible ships he pilots hurry on?
The very ocean sees that his will's done.
His little finger moving moves these swarms
of dragons, countless black and wingèd forms.
The king has spoken: terrible man of shade,
and all his mass of monsters has obeyed.
At Cairo's mosque, when the Bey Cifresil
sank the great wells, he carved this on a wall:
'To Allah heaven, but the earth to me.'
And, as all things are one at last, we see
all tyrants are one tyrant. Time retrieves,
and what the sultan said, this king believes.

Meanwhile, in wonder at the basin's rim,
the Infanta holds her rose, from time to time
kissing it—blue-eyed angel that she is!
Suddenly a breath, the kind of skirmishing breeze
that sometimes leaps at dusk across the plains,
troubles the water, bends the rushes, runs
crazily through the daffodils and myrtles,
comes to the musing little girl, and hurtles
upon her. The trees shudder. And the wind
scatters her flower's petals to the pond.

The Infanta clutches at a stalk of thorn.
Stooping, she sees her treasure tossed and torn.
She does not understand. She is afraid.
She looks up at the sky, her face dismayed,
seeking the breeze that risked displeasing her.
What can she do? Anger is all astir
in the pure pool, making it black with waves.
And now it is a sea that boils and heaves.
And now the pitiful flower is dispersed,
its hundred petals, horribly immersed,
whirling in terrible shipwreck everywhere
through water clapping to the rowdy air.

434

It might have been a fleet of sinking ships.

'Madame'—the guardian's thin, tutorial lips
instruct the little girl's astonished mind:
'All things belong to princes but the wind.'

1952; 1957–August 10, 1959

Biographical Note

In October, 1906, Dilys, the first child of Alfred James and Eve Bennett, was born in Pwllheli, North Wales. His work as a civil engineer took Mr. Bennett to places remote from the centers of civilization, and when possible his family accompanied him. The first of these journeys, to the north of Scotland, came when Dilys was less than a year old. After a few months, the family moved south, to Weymouth, England. Here she spent five years while her father, away on the coast of Nigeria, helped to build the port of Lagos. It was at Weymouth that her brother John was born, and as he grew, he and Dilys became devoted companions.

The day after her second birthday, Dilys came down with polio. The case was a serious one, and for a time there was little hope that she would be able to walk without a brace. Yet the patience and determination of her mother, who encouraged and assisted Dilys to exercise the afflicted leg, gradually brought strength back to it. Eventually, only a residual weakness remained, and Dilys took pleasure in long walks for the rest of her life.

The profoundest effect of the disease was not physical but psychological. As she recovered from the illness, she led a life that was more sheltered than that of most children. She was spared the painful give and take of childhood, and when she finally came to face the realities of the world as an adult the shock was all the greater. Though she often regretted having been cloistered as a child, the poetic vision that allowed her to see where civilization has failed to preserve harmony in the world probably had its origin in this contrast.

Upon his return from Africa, A. J. Bennett moved his family to the city of Port Arthur, Ontario. At that time, Dilys was six and a half. Two years later, in 1915, the Bennetts moved again, this time to Vancouver, British Columbia, where they

435

Biographical Note

lived for six years. Because of these frequent changes in residence, her isolation within her family persisted through the years that most children spend in public school. She was educated privately by governesses, tutors, and music and art teachers.

At the age of two and a half, she had begun to amuse her mother by talking in rhyme, a game which she continued until, at twelve, she began to contribute little poems and children's stories, many of them illustrated by her own drawings, to Canadian and American newspapers and magazines. In 1918, she became seriously ill again. A mastoid infection required delicate surgery that left her nearly deaf in one ear, but with a hurtful sensitivity to some sounds. A long convalescence gave her time to write, draw, and read, and once again an affliction was turned to advantage.

Among the newspapers to which Dilys contributed was the *Vancouver Daily Sun,* in which there was a Sunday page for children. Dilys, at fourteen, was appointed editor of the page, and she continued in this capacity for two years until the family moved to Victoria. Four years later, in 1925, she joined the editorial staff of the *Victoria Daily Colonist.*

In 1926, at the age of twenty, Dilys went with her mother to Europe for two years to study art and languages. In London, she worked under the guidance of Professor Tonks at the Slade School of Art. Returning to North America in 1928, Dilys and Mrs. Bennett rejoined their family in Seattle, where they lived for eight years. As time passed, Dilys neglected her drawing and painting and concentrated instead upon her writing. From all evidences, she began to define the role for herself to which she would remain committed thereafter. She was encouraged to do so by Bliss Carman, a family friend.

Dilys spent the summer of 1928 in Gray's Harbor, Washington, where her father was supervising the construction of a pulp mill. There she encountered Idella Purnell, editor of the poetry magazine *Palms,* to which, with the issue of the following January, she became a contributor. My father, Alexander Laing, had had several poems in earlier issues of *Palms,* and as a consequence had been invited by its pub-

436

lisher for a visit on the coast of Washington. He found a job on a freighter bound from Newark, New Jersey, to southern California. After an adventurous trek up the coast, he reached Gray's Harbor early in July. Alex and Dilys met there and became very close in spite of family tensions arising from his unconcern, as a young writer, over his financial prospects. When he returned to the east coast he wrote to Dilys, but her replies were noncommittal. A year and a half later, he married Isabel Lattimore, from whom he was divorced in 1934.

Shortly afterward, he began a year-long journey around the world on a Guggenheim Fellowship. He wrote to Dilys from Honolulu, asking whether he should take the route to New York by way of San Francisco or Seattle. Dilys's reply, by cable, was "Seattle." They were married there on May 30, 1936. Then they moved to Vermont, where they built their home on nine acres of partly wooded land in the hills west of Norwich bought from Will Bond, a farmer, who served as prototype for the hero of a novel she wrote a decade later.

I was born in August, 1940. Dilys was very ill after my birth, and she was warned not to have any more children. Perhaps that was just as well, since it was at this time that she began her greatest struggle with domesticity and its restrictions on her life as a creative artist. A few months after her marriage she had written in her diary:

> As for me—I'd rather be a writer than what I must
> be. Housework exasperates me. I had hoped that
> I might discover in myself undeveloped veins of
> domesticity, but alas, I hate it.

Several of her poems of the latter 1930's show nevertheless her determination to identify herself with the New England culture. Shortly after the publication of her first book, entitled with deliberate ambivalence *Another England*, she became in December, 1941, a citizen of the United States.

Dilys had no patience with artificialities, nor had she any for those acquaintances who welcomed, or at least admitted, artificialities into their lives. Her moments of insight were the fruit of aloneness and meditation. She regarded intruders into this state as murderers, and she confronted the intrusions with vitriolic temper. Material possessions and their contingent demands were as much intruders, in her view, as any humans. No less to be cursed than dirty clothes and dishes were the mechanisms by which they were restored to function. The life of an ascetic would have suited Dilys's personality exquisitely, had it been possible for her to follow it.

Dilys's attitude toward technological progress, an emergent concern in her second book, *Birth Is Farewell* (1944), was in close agreement with her feelings about modern conveniences. She was imbued with a sense of a proper order in nature, and of man's subordinate place within the scheme. It was bitter to her to observe the inexorable progression of inventions that remove people ever further from what she believed was their wholesome dependence upon the natural world. In Dilys's view, man divorced from nature becomes a dead thing, as much so as a leaf divorced from its tree. The person of Sam Potter, the Vermont farmer in her novel, *The Great Year*, embodies the ideal of man living in harmony with the earth that gave him life:

> The fire of the trees, burning over the hills and the valleys as far as the sky-colored mountains, administered to his nerves once again its annual long shock of pleasure. Every year this beauty entered him, falling, itself like a leaf, upon the growing pile of its past self, or perhaps rather like a transparent image of fall, fixing itself upon past images to make one fall, to make one season of all autumns, one year of all years. This sense of wholeness, of having come full circle back to an experience, was a truth that Sam could not adequately realize in images or express in words, but it was the reality that robbed time of its power to pass and take all strength and sweetness with it in its passing. It was the reality of recurrence, the reassurance of pattern without which time would be indeed only a sequence and humanity only an incident. The fact that autumn returned and would again return gave Sam the strength, the calm, the hope he needed to forgive himself his own sins and grow, not in a long thin line of extension, but like a tree, upward, downward, outward, circle on circle.

438

Biographical Note

We had a large print of Pieter Breughel's painting of the fall of Icarus hanging in our house. This painting served our family as the symbol of the danger to mankind of a persistent dependence upon the wax wings of technology. This symbolic sense is present in *The Great Year*, as Della gives her brother Sam a copy of the painting. For Dilys the most alarming element of the new technology was of course the nuclear bomb. After the bombing of Hiroshima, she made the immediate moral judgment: "Oh, that was evil!"

Although she did not seek opportunities to read in public, she generally accepted invitations to do so. In March of 1945 she read at Harvard, and as a consequence was invited by Dudley Fitts, a month later, to Phillips Andover Academy. In the following February she spent a week at Saint Mary's in the Mountains, at Littleton, New Hampshire, guiding the creative efforts of students. The poem "Assignment" (page 246) was one outcome of this experience. Shortly afterward she was asked by John Holmes to deliver the 1946 Phi Beta Kappa poem at Tufts College. Although not inclined to write poetry for occasions, she was already at work upon her condemnation of atomic testing, "Not One Atoll," and so used it for the purpose. A quotation:

> This is my father's and my mother's home.
> Do it no harm, I love it. It is mine.
> I charge you not for any frivolous reason
> of curiosity or greed or fear
> to scar it anywhere. Do not hurt one island,
> no, not the littlest atoll, in the name
> of science or security. I say:
> This is my Father's house. Behave yourselves.

In 1946 Dilys was shaken by the death of a younger cousin, Monica Roberts Chalmers, whose own promise as a poet made the loss doubly meaningful. "Clear Specter (*For Mona*)"—the dedicatory poem of *Walk Through Two Landscapes*—was many months in the writing and is a drastic compression of a much longer manuscript form. "Last Discipline" (page 290) was at one point in the making a part of "Clear Specter."

Biographical Note

The sacrifice of children in an uncompassionate world is a recurrent theme in Dilys's writing, for example in the poem "Fertility Rite." She believed as a principle and not as an easy sentiment that the salvation and preservation of the world is always in the hands of the young, and she was unhappy with the woeful state of things that her generation had to pass on to its children. "Forgive me," she said in a poem addressed to me,

> for neglecting to show you
> that the world is evil.
> I had hoped your innocence would find it good
> and teach me what I know to be untrue.

She rejected the harsher ways of preparing a child to make its own peace with the world. Home was a pleasant haven for me, never a place of fear or opprobrium. All through my childhood, Dilys guided my senses in their regard of nature. Despite the weakened leg that she inherited from her youth, she took whatever chance she could to walk with me briskly in the Vermont countryside. The hills rise behind our house, unbroken by the artificial works of civilization. Here we would pass through the woods, quietly looking, listening, and waiting, and the finding of each new wonder was the making of another bond between the humans we were and the real world from which we were evolved. I was still very young when I came to know that the differences between myself and a squirrel were only matters of variation on a grand theme of which all natural things are parts. We were infused with a sense of belonging within a motivating, cyclic harmony to which the actions of all physical things are responses.

It was hard for Dilys to accept traditional views of religion. And yet her skepticism never caused her to reject traditional religions in their entirety. She believed in the message and the person of Jesus Christ, and her poetry is rich with the imagery taken from the story of his life and death. "A Common Tree" compresses into its six lines her belief that Jesus, all questions of his divinity aside, was among the best of *men.* The poem, originally of thirty lines, is an example of her constant search for the essence of her themes.

440

Biographical Note

Dilys rarely went to church, preferring her own mind to a sectarian temple for the contemplation of metaphysics. She drew not only upon Christianity, but upon other religions as well in the formulation of her own philosophy. The Eastern religions were of particular interest to her, Tao and Zen being closest to her ways of thinking about man and Nature. But I think of her own philosophy as being more created than eclectic. From the philosophies of others she sought strength rather than inspiration.

Sometimes, when the news was full of disaster, Dilys saw fit to blame God for complacency, as in "Final Verdict." In this poem, and in others, notably "I-Thou," a theme of agnosticism emerges. Dilys, not completely content with philosophy based upon order in nature, leaned toward the more traditional idea of an intelligent creator. But she was not satisfied that God should be the image of man, or even that God should be *masculine*, for she says in "Let Them Ask Their Husbands,"

> . . . God created
> woman in Her own image
> and I have
> my Pauline pride.

After World War II, a number of the poets who were rebuilding a free German culture showed a marked interest in Dilys's work. Her two long poems both appeared in the new magazine *Prisma:* "Elegy for an Engineer" was reprinted in English with a German translation by Ina Seidel, in August, 1947; "Not One Atoll" followed, in a translation by Dora Lubach, again with the English original in parallel columns. Other translators included Masha Kaleko and Fritz Volquard Arnold. She had also published several short stories, one of which was translated into German.

Dilys's only published novel, *The Great Year*, came out in 1948; it was reissued six years later in Hans Hennecke's German translation. A third book of poems, *Walk Through Two Landscapes*, appeared in 1949. She had been highly productive in the 1940's: four books and nearly one hundred and fifty magazine appearances. The comparative silence of the following decade calls for an explanation. It is partly to be accounted for by a profound change in subject matter and therefore in style, partly by a shift of interest to two ambitious prose works involving difficult and prolonged research, partly by longer and longer periods of sickness. Her intense anguish over the sacrifice of youth in war, which had been ameliorated at least a little by her view that the allied aims of World War II were honorable, got no such support as the threats of the atomic era deepened.

In 1940 Archibald MacLeish had published in *The Nation* an essay titled "The Irresponsibles" reproaching those who choose to look the other way while their world is being perverted by their own species. Ten years later, believing the Cold War was erasing all claims to a moral gain from victory in World War II, Dilys and Alex organized a group they called "The Responsibles." Together, they wrote a "Letter to a Threatened World," which likewise appeared in *The Nation.* This "Letter," together with an accompanying "Declaration of the Concerned," was privately printed and circulated by "The Responsibles." The chain-letter response throughout the nation was enormous. Dilys soon found herself doing little else than the clerical work of dealing with innumerable letters. She had to turn the task over to local volunteers in order to return to her central work, her writing. Nevertheless the episode confirmed her in a poet's confrontation of the sternest issues of her era. Her acceptance of the role of Cassandra in the Dartmouth production of the *Agamemnon* in January, 1951, had for Dilys a deliberate inference.

About a month later the three of us headed south by car to spend Alex's sabbatical semester in Mexico, an experience which profoundly changed the remainder of Dilys's creative life. She found the country beautiful and terrifying, the people friendly and heartbreaking, and everywhere the symbol of the skull. The Mexican poems in this book reflect her combined love and dismay. "Dance of Burros" signals the end of one era in her artistry, the beginning of another. *The New Yorker* accepted it, but asked to change what she regarded as its finest line. She refused, and returned a much needed check.

442

Biographical Note

The poem later appeared unchanged in *Poetry*; but *The New Yorker*, which had published thirty-one of her poems, never accepted another. The reason was at least partly related to her choice of sterner subjects.

After our return from Mexico, informal but fairly frequent poetry evenings became a habit in our house. Those regularly attending, at one time or another, included the poets Philip Booth, Thomas and Vera Vance, Bink Noll, Ramon Guthrie, Ned O'Gorman, Frederic Will, and Richard Eberhart. For a year, beginning in the fall of 1952, Dilys had a half-time post overseeing the browsing room of the college library. She did this partly to earn money to pay for domestic help, partly for access in the mornings to a library study for research into a major project—a novel about the confrontation of two devoted priests in an irreconcilable clash of cultures, Spanish and Aztec. Voluminous records of her labor toward this partly finished work survive: an analytical vocabulary of the Nahuatl language, of which she taught herself enough to read the early transliterated codices, many notebooks on her anthropological and historical reading, and a number of draft chapters which eventually brought a modest option payment from Macmillan, in the year before her death.

The deepening cycle of periods of ill health caused her to resign her library job, which however had brought her many enduring undergraduate friendships. She continued, when physically able, to work with the Players. The collapse of a stage prop in Henry IV, Part 1, in which she was Lady Percy, sent her to the hospital for Christmas, 1953. In 1955 she played Grace Winslow in *The Winslow Boy*, and in January of 1959 had a happy last stage appearance in a musical comedy, *The Boy Friend*.

A task which caused her even more distress than the merciless Aztec researches had origins that appear in her journal entry for June 22, 1953:

> D. & I went on to talk of ideas of good & evil, & I
> found myself telling him a fable which I do believe
> would make a fine novella. The story of a doctor deliv-
> ering with great difficulty a remarkably well made

443

baby boy. The mother is a sick & destitute, unknown
woman, with remains of great beauty. It is a breach
birth & the doctor cannot imagine why it is so difficult
to bring the child out until he discovers to his horror
that it has two heads. It's body is so beautiful that he
has struggled hard to save its life. . . . it upsets all
expectations by flourishing & growing to manhood.
The two heads are named Dexter & Sinister—& are
radically different in all their ideas. Dexter is a libertine & philistine, plays the saxophone—sleeps with the
girls—loves all pleasures—has a sunny nature—a
pagan. Sinister is an ascetic & would be a monk if that
were possible. . . . Sinister has to endure all Dexter's
pleasures & his greatest trial is to avoid enjoying
them. . . . Left & right have no political significance.

There is the suggestion of a subconscious origin, twelve years
earlier, in the fourth stanza of "Drink-Me" (page 243).

The fate of this story, which she called *Corazón*, obsessed
her throughout the rest of her life. She rewrote it several times,
with notes of growing desperation over it entered frequently
in her journals. Three publishers of other books of hers reported simply that they did not dare to print it, although editors at Macmillan recalled it twice for new attempts to per-
suade their colleagues. Dilys regarded *Corazón* as a central,
symbolic statement of the schizophrenia of her era. Despite
her initial denial of political intent, the story became her own
ultimate comment upon East-and-West Germany, North-and-
South Korea, and all the other instances of man's fateful need
to share nevertheless the single body of his humanity.

Corazón's double life reflected, of course, her own, her
swing between gaiety and utter despair. She enjoyed sailing.
"Aquitation" reflects the pleasure she took in her rating of
"Skipper, Class 2," attained in July of 1955, at the Dartmouth
Sailing Club. One of her moments of purest delight came on
a misty day when we sailed out of Nantucket harbor toward
a horizon blooming with scores of colorful spinnakers of the
New York Yacht Club's cruise. On March 3, 1955, she read her
poem "Smoking Mirror" before the Brown University chapter
of Phi Beta Kappa at its celebration of its 125th anniversary.
On this occasion, although she had never been enrolled in an

institution of higher learning, she was made an honorary member of the society, entitled to wear its key.

Partly because of her British-American background, she was invited to be the poet to read at the Poetry Society of Virginia's celebration of the 350th anniversary, in October, 1957, of the first permanent English settlement in America. On the way home she spent two rewarding days with her beloved friends, the M. L. Rosenthals.

She began to write light verse again, but it did not sell. On March 11, 1958, she wrote:

> These refusals don't hurt me much—The poems are
> trivial—though done for the joy of words—but
> they don't count—& Corazón does.

A diary entry on her only meeting with Marianne Moore, a month later, reveals the humility that had come from her disappointments.

> When I was introduced, she said, "I didn't know I was
> going to meet you!" I think I blushed. "You don't
> mean to say that you really know my work!" I said in
> real astonishment, & she replied—"Of *course* I do! . . .
> *You* ought to have been reading to *me*." . . . she
> really did know some of my poems. . . . she said, as if
> regretfully—"Sometimes you are too mournful—" —
> "Perhaps angry rather than mournful," I suggested—
> "Yes—angry—" she agreed, & seemed better pleased
> with that idea. . . . At the all-too-soon end of the
> evening I asked her to write in my copy of her little
> book, Nevertheless. She wrote . . . "To Dilys Laing
> (and she knew how to spell it!) I wish I were giving
> you more than a signature." I didn't tell her that she
> had, pressed down & running over. . . .

As a relief from her Aztec researches she returned to the discipline of translation, chiefly from Prévert and Hugo. In the spring of 1959 she lamented that she had "sent nothing anywhere but to the *Nation* for ages—they have printed 11 poems in 15 months. I *really* haven't felt well." Her health returned enough, with the summer, for us to visit the Eberharts in Maine. There was a side trip to Castine for a lobster dinner with the Philip Booths and the Robert Lowells. Upon our return Dilys was well enough to begin organizing an application for a Guggenheim Fellowship which she hoped might take her to Spain in the following year for the completion of her Spanish-Aztec novel. We also at this time were reading, in the family, such Greek plays as the *Alcestis* and the *Agamemnon*, preludes to my elected fall-term course in classical civilization. On August 2 a letter of acceptance arrived from Macmillan, of the manuscript of *Poems from a Cage*. But in the midst of these hopeful signs an affliction for which Dilys had been receiving allergy tests and treatments worsened. We thought it related to the hay fever season, but it did not lessen with the frost. On October 28 she wrote of ". . . a fit of coughing so strangling that I was more than ever convinced that I have asthma. . . ." After a visit to the hospital she added, ". . . it is asthma. . . . It is costing too much in drugs to keep me alive."

With the preceding day's entry she had decided, "From now on, David, I think I'll let my diary take the form of a continuous letter to you. . . . I could direct it to Alex—but . . . you are away from both of us—& we miss you so." The following pages seem to be a tranquil ordering of her thoughts, as if she knew what was soon to happen.

A preoccupation with her own involvement, as if she were responsible for the world's injustice and cruelty, visited her often as she approached her final illness, and perhaps made it inevitable. She may really have died of grief. But it was her nature, even after the worst times but the last one, to swing widely toward a fleeting joy, at least toward calm.

Dilys divided her only published novel into the twelve chapters of the eternal year. Each of these is a complete episode in itself, yet all are united by the theme of returning: the "wholeness of having come back full circle to an experience." In her life and in her poems I find the same sense of wholeness, a constant turning again to compassion, to aloneness, to the natural world.

During her last autumn she reread *Anna Karenina* ("after 15 yrs. or so—this time much more impressive"), *The Ordeal of Richard Feverel*, and Castiglione, but most of all in Saint Augustine: *The Confessions* and *The City of God*. Her notes

446

on the latter fill a sizable blank book. She spent most of November in the hospital, and returned for several weeks of home care, but was back in the Mary Hitchcock Memorial Hospital on January 31, 1960. She died there of an acute attack of asthma, shortly before dawn on February 14.

She had with her in her room a small blank book. The poem that follows is written on its final page: probably her last first draft.

DAVID BENNETT LAING

Plan Ahead

I have been long away
from the electric hills
locked in my own anatomy.

The brain's a stuffy attic.
Here I've foraged
a long while out of the sun.

chewing the old clothes
of scholarship, a dry moth.
Now I fly through the window.

This is the way moths die:
drowned by the sun
or snapped up by a humming bird.

So be it.

Index of Titles and First Lines

449

Index of Titles and First Lines

Index of Titles and First Lines

451

Index of Titles and First Lines

Index of Titles and First Lines

454

Index of Titles and First Lines

Index of Titles and First Lines

456

Index of Titles and First Lines

457

Index of Titles and First Lines

Index of Titles and First Lines

Index of Titles and First Lines

Index of Titles and First Lines

461

Index of Titles and First Lines

Index of Titles and First Lines

Index of Titles and First Lines